# ENGAGE & CONVERT

## ADVANCED CONTENT MARKETING TECHNIQUES

Strategies for Engaging, Converting and Retaining Audiences

**NATHAN SHEWRING**

Copyright © 2024 by Nathan Shewring
All rights reserved. This book or any portion thereof
may not be reproduced or used in any manner whatsoever
without the express written permission of the publisher
except for the use of brief quotations in a book review.

The right of Nathan Shewring to be identified as author of this work has been asserted by him in accordance with the Copyright, Designs and Patents Act 1988.

First Edition

Editor: Garry Shewring

For My Family

# Contents

**Chapter 1: Introduction ................................................................. 1**

    I. The Importance of Audience Engagement in Content Marketing ...... 1

        A. Defining Audience Engagement and Its Significance ..................... 1

        B. The Shift from Traditional Marketing to Content Marketing .......... 2

        C. Why Audience Engagement Matters More Than Ever ................. 3

    II. Setting the Stage: The Landscape of Content Marketing ................. 5

        A. Evolution of Content Marketing: From Print to Digital ................. 5

        B. Current Trends and Challenges in Content Marketing.................. 7

        C. Opportunities for Brands in Engaging Audiences Through Content ........................................................................................... 8

    III. Objectives and Structure of the Book ............................................. 11

        A. Overview of the Book's Purpose and Goals ................................ 11

        B. Explanation of the Book's Organisation and Flow ...................... 12

        C. What Readers Can Expect to Gain from Each Chapter................. 14

    IV. Who This Book Is For ...................................................................... 16

        A. Target Audience: Marketing Professionals, Business Owners, and Content Creators ........................................................................ 16

        B. How This Book Can Benefit Readers in Different Roles and Industries................................................................................................ 18

        C. Why Audience Engagement Is Relevant Across Various Sectors . 20

    V. How to Use This Book .................................................................... 21

        A. Guide to Navigating Through Chapters and Sections .................. 22

        B. Suggestions for Active Engagement and Application of Strategies ............................................................................................ 23

        C. Resources and Tools Recommended Throughout the Book ........ 25

    VI. Meet the Author ............................................................................ 26

A. Background and Expertise in Technology and the Digital World.................................................................................................26

B. Inspiration Behind Writing the Book............................................27

VII. Conclusion..................................................................................27

A. Recap of Key Points Covered in the Introduction ........................27

B. Anticipation of What's to Come in the Subsequent Chapters .....28

C. Encouragement for Readers to Dive into the Content and Begin Their Journey Toward Mastering Content Marketing Strategies for Engaging Audiences. ..........................................................29

## Chapter 2: Understanding Your Audience ...............................30

I. Introduction to Understanding Your Audience ...................................30

A. Importance of Audience Understanding in Content Marketing ..30

B. Overview of Chapter Objectives and Structure............................30

II. Identifying Target Audience Segments ............................................31

A. Demographic Analysis...................................................................31

B. Psychographic Profiling .................................................................31

C. Behavioural Segmentation ............................................................31

D. Customer Surveys and Feedback .................................................32

III. Creating Audience Personas...........................................................32

A. Definition and Purpose of Audience Personas............................32

B. Steps for Developing Audience Personas....................................32

C. Examples of Effective Audience Personas...................................33

IV. Conducting Audience Research .....................................................34

A. Methods for Gathering Audience Data.........................................34

B. Analysing Audience Insights.........................................................35

C. Tools and Resources for Audience Research ..............................36

V. Understanding Audience Needs and Preferences .........................37

A. Identifying Pain Points and Challenges .......................................37

B. Assessing Content Preferences and Formats ...................................38

C. Addressing Audience Needs Through Content Solutions.............39

VI. Leveraging Audience Insights for Content Creation ........................40

A. Tailoring Content Messaging and Tone ........................................40

B. Creating Content that Resonates with Audience Segments ........41

C. Incorporating Audience Feedback and Iterating Content Strategies ..................................................................................................42

VII. Testing and Optimisation ..................................................................43

A. A/B Testing Content Variations......................................................43

B. Analysing Content Performance Metrics ......................................44

C. Iterating Content Strategies Based on Insights ............................45

VIII. Case Studies and Examples ............................................................46

A. Real-World Examples of Audience Understanding in Action .......46

B. Case Studies Highlighting Successful Audience-Centric Content Marketing Campaigns ...........................................................................48

IX. Conclusion............................................................................................49

A. Recap of Key Insights and Takeaways..........................................49

B. Importance of Ongoing Audience Understanding in Content Marketing Strategy.................................................................................50

C. Next Steps for Applying Audience Insights to Content Marketing Efforts ...................................................................................51

## Chapter 3: Crafting Compelling Content.........................................53

I. Introduction to Crafting Compelling Content ....................................53

A. Overview of the Chapter's Purpose ...............................................53

B. Importance of Compelling Content in Audience Engagement.....53

II. Understanding Content Psychology..................................................55

A. The Psychology of Content Consumption ....................................55

B. Leveraging Emotional Triggers in Content Creation .....................56

C. Cognitive Biases and Their Impact on Content Effectiveness ....... 56
III. Storytelling Techniques for Engaging Audiences ............................ 57
    A. The Power of Storytelling in Content Marketing ........................ 57
    B. Elements of Effective Storytelling .................................................. 58
    C. Incorporating Narrative Arcs in Content Creation ...................... 59
IV. Content Formats and Delivery Channels.......................................... 60
    A. Exploring Different Content Formats (e.g., Articles, Videos, Infographics) ............................................................................................ 60
    B. Choosing the Right Delivery Channels for Your Audience............ 61
    C. Multichannel Content Distribution Strategies ........................... 62
V. Writing Compelling Copy and Headlines........................................... 63
    A. Crafting Attention-Grabbing Headlines ....................................... 63
    B. Writing Persuasive Copy that Drives Action................................ 63
    C. Tips for Optimising Copy for SEO and Readability ...................... 64
VI. Visual Content Creation Strategies .................................................. 65
    A. Importance of Visual Content in Audience Engagement ............. 65
    B. Design Principles for Creating Visually Compelling Content ........ 66
    C. Tools and Resources for Creating Visual Content ....................... 66
VII. Personalised Content Strategies ..................................................... 67
    A. Understanding the Importance of Personalised Content ............ 67
    B. Strategies for Segmenting Audiences for Personalisation ........... 68
    C. Dynamic Content Creation Techniques........................................ 69
VIII. Content Repurposing and Curation ............................................... 70
    A. Leveraging Existing Content for Audience Engagement .............. 70
    B. Best Practices for Content Curation............................................. 70
    C. Strategies for Repurposing Content Across Different Channels .. 71
IX. User-Generated Content Strategies................................................. 72

    A. Harnessing the Power of User-Generated Content ..................... 72

    B. Encouraging User Participation and Engagement ....................... 72

    C. Moderation and Management of User-Generated Content ........ 73

  X. Content Performance Measurement and Optimisation .................. 74

    A. Key Metrics for Evaluating Content Performance ...................... 74

    B. Tools and Analytics Platforms for Content Measurement ........... 75

    C. Iterative Optimisation Based on Performance Insights ............... 75

  XI. Conclusion: Applying Content Strategies ........................................ 76

    A. Recap of Key Insights and Strategies ........................................ 76

    B. Encouragement for Applying Techniques in Content Creation .... 77

    C. Looking Ahead to Implementing Content Strategies in the Next Chapters .................................................................................. 78

## Chapter 4: Leveraging Distribution Channels ........................... 79

  I. Introduction to Distribution Channels ............................................... 79

    A. Definition and Importance ......................................................... 79

    B. Overview of Distribution Channel Types .................................... 79

  II. Understanding Distribution Channel Options ................................. 80

    A. Owned Channels ...................................................................... 80

    B. Earned Channels ...................................................................... 82

    C. Paid Channels ........................................................................... 82

  III. Tailoring Content for Different Distribution Channels ..................... 83

    A. Content Formats and Messaging .............................................. 83

    B. Optimisation Techniques .......................................................... 85

  IV. Developing a Distribution Channel Strategy .................................. 87

    A. Audience Analysis and Channel Selection ................................ 87

    B. Content Calendar and Publishing Schedule .............................. 88

    C. Integration and Cross-Promotion Strategies .............................. 89

V. Measuring and Analysing Distribution Channel Performance ........ 90

   A. Key Performance Indicators (KPIs) ............................................... 90

   B. Analytics Tools and Platforms ....................................................... 92

VI. Optimisation and Iteration ................................................................ 94

   A. Continuous Monitoring and Analysis .......................................... 94

   B. Iterative Testing and Refinement ................................................. 94

   C. Adaptation to Changing Trends and Audience Preferences ........ 95

VII. Success in Distribution Channel Strategies ................................... 96

   A. Successful Distribution Channel Strategies ................................ 96

   B. Lessons Learned and Best Practices ............................................. 97

VIII. Conclusion: Maximising Distribution Channel Strategies ............ 98

   A. Recap of Distribution Channel Strategies ................................... 98

   B. Encouragement for Implementation and Experimentation ....... 98

   C. Looking Ahead to Further Refinement and Growth .................... 99

**Chapter 5: Fostering Community Engagement ........................ 100**

   I. Introduction to Community Engagement ..................................... 100

     A. Definition and Importance of Community Engagement ............ 100

     B. Benefits of Building a Community Around Your Brand ............. 100

     C. Overview of Chapter Objectives and Structure .......................... 101

   II. Understanding Your Community ................................................. 102

     A. Identifying and Defining Your Target Community ..................... 102

     B. Analysing Community Needs, Interests, and Behaviours ........... 103

     C. Segmenting Your Community for Personalised Engagement .... 103

   III. Building and Nurturing Community Relationships ...................... 104

     A. Establishing Trust and Credibility ................................................ 104

     B. Creating Valuable Content for Community Members ............... 105

     C. Encouraging Participation and Interaction ................................. 105

IV. Leveraging Community Platforms and Tools ................................. 106

   A. Choosing the Right Community Platforms (e.g., social media, forums, online groups) ........................................................................ 106

   B. Implementing Community Management Best Practices ........... 107

   C. Utilising Community Engagement Tools and Analytics ............. 107

V. Measuring and Analysing Community Engagement ...................... 108

   A. Key Metrics for Evaluating Community Engagement ................ 109

   B. Analytics Tools and Platforms for Community Analysis ............. 109

   C. Continuous Monitoring and Adaptation Strategies ................... 110

VI. Cultivating a Culture of Engagement ............................................ 111

   A. Encouraging User-Generated Content and Contributions ......... 111

   B. Facilitating Meaningful Discussions and Interactions ................ 112

   C. Empowering Community Advocates and Brand Ambassadors .. 112

VII. Case Studies and Examples of Successful Community Engagement ........................................................................................ 113

   A. Real-World Examples of Brands Fostering Community Engagement ........................................................................................ 113

   B. Lessons Learned and Best Practices from Community Engagement Success Stories .............................................................. 114

VIII. Conclusion: Building Stronger Community Connections ........... 115

   A. Recap of Key Insights and Strategies ......................................... 115

   B. Encouragement for Implementing Community Engagement Tactics ................................................................................................. 116

   C. Looking Ahead to Building Stronger Community Connections .. 116

**Chapter 6: Measuring and Analysing Engagement ................... 117**

   I. Introduction to Measuring Engagement ....................................... 117

      A. Importance of Measuring Engagement ................................. 117

      B. Overview of Chapter Objectives ............................................. 117

II. Key Metrics for Evaluating Engagement .................................................. 118
   A. Definition and Significance of Engagement Metrics .................. 118
   B. Types of Engagement Metrics .................................................... 119
III. Analytics Tools and Platforms .................................................................. 121
   A. Google Analytics ........................................................................ 121
   B. Social Media Analytics ............................................................... 122
   C. Content Management Systems (CMS) ...................................... 123
   D. Email Marketing Platforms ......................................................... 124
   E. Customer Relationship Management (CRM) Systems ............... 124
IV. Setting Up Measurement Frameworks ..................................................... 125
   A. Establishing Goals and Objectives ............................................ 125
   B. Defining Key Performance Indicators (KPIs) ............................. 126
   C. Implementing Tracking and Tagging ......................................... 127
V. Interpreting and Analysing Data ................................................................ 127
   A. Data Visualisation Techniques .................................................. 127
   B. Identifying Trends and Patterns ................................................ 128
   C. Understanding Audience Behaviour ......................................... 129
VI. Continuous Monitoring and Adaptation .................................................... 130
   A. Importance of Ongoing Analysis ............................................... 130
   B. Iterative Optimisation Strategies ............................................... 131
   C. Adaptation to Changing Trends ................................................ 131
VII. Real-World Measurement Practices ........................................................ 132
   A. Real-World Examples of Effective Measurement Practices ...... 132
   B. Lessons Learned and Best Practices from Success Stories ..... 133
VIII. Conclusion: Maximising Engagement through Effective
Measurement ................................................................................................. 134
   A. Recap of Key Insights and Strategies ....................................... 134

B. Encouragement for Implementing Measurement Tactics .........135

   C. Looking Ahead to Enhanced Engagement Strategies................135

**Chapter 7: Personalisation in Content Marketing .....................137**

   I. Introduction to Personalisation ......................................................137

      A. Audience Segmentation and Profiling ........................................137

      B. Data Collection and Analysis for Personalisation......................137

      C. Leveraging Audience Insights for Tailored Experiences ............138

   II. Understanding Your Audience for Personalisation ........................138

      A. Audience Segmentation and Profiling ........................................138

      B. Data Collection and Analysis for Personalisation......................139

      C. Leveraging Audience Insights for Tailored Experiences ............140

   III Implementing Personalisation Tactics ...........................................140

      A. Dynamic Content Creation Techniques .....................................140

      B. Customising Content Messaging and Tone ................................141

      C. Adaptive Content Delivery Across Channels ..............................141

   IV. Tools and Technologies for Personalisation...................................142

      A. Content Management Systems (CMS)........................................142

      B. Customer Relationship Management (CRM) Software..............142

      C. Marketing Automation Platforms ..............................................143

   V. Measuring the Impact of Personalisation ......................................144

      A. Key Performance Indicators (KPIs) for Personalisation............144

      B. Analytics Tools and Metrics .......................................................144

      C. Continuous Optimisation Based on Performance Insights.........145

   VI. Real-World Case Studies and Examples .......................................146

      A. Successful Personalisation Strategies in Action .......................146

      B. Lessons Learned and Best Practices from Industry Leaders ......146

   VII. Challenges and Considerations in Personalisation.......................147

 A. Privacy and Data Security Concerns............................................147

 B. Balancing Personalisation with User Experience .......................147

 C. Overcoming Implementation Challenges....................................148

VIII. Future Trends and Opportunities in Personalisation ..................149

 A. Emerging Technologies and Innovations ...................................149

 B. The Future of Personalised Content Experiences ......................149

 C. Strategies for Staying Ahead in a Personalised Landscape ........150

## Chapter 8: Cultivating Long-Term Relationships........................151

I. Introduction to Long-Term Relationship Building in Content Marketing....................................................................................................151

 A. Importance of Long-Term Relationships for Audience Engagement ...............................................................................................151

 B. Shift from Transactional to Relational Marketing......................151

 C. Benefits of Building Customer Loyalty and Advocacy ................152

II. Understanding Customer Needs and Preferences ..........................152

 A. Customer Journey Mapping and Lifecycle Analysis ...................152

 B. Listening to Customer Feedback and Sentiment Analysis..........153

 C. Creating Personas for Targeted Relationship Building...............153

III. Strategies for Building Trust and Credibility...................................154

 A. Providing Value-Driven Content and Resources ........................154

 B. Transparency and Authenticity in Communication....................155

 C. Building Social Proof and Reputation Management ..................155

IV. Nurturing Relationships Through Personalisation .......................156

 A. Tailoring Content and Experiences to Individual Preferences ...156

 B. Leveraging Data to Anticipate Customer Needs ........................156

 C. Implementing Lifecycle Marketing Strategies............................157

V. Communication and Engagement Tactics.......................................157

 A. Effective Email Marketing Strategies for Relationship Building.157

 B. Social Media Engagement and Community Building ................. 158

 C. Interactive Content and Conversational Marketing .................. 158

VI. Customer Service and Support ....................................................... 159

 A. Providing Exceptional Customer Service Experiences .............. 159

 B. Addressing Customer Concerns and Resolving Issues Promptly 160

 C. Turning Customer Feedback into Opportunities for Improvement ........................................................................................ 160

VII. Loyalty Programs and Incentives ................................................. 161

 A. Designing Loyalty Programs to Reward and Retain Customers . 161

 B. Offering Exclusive Benefits and Incentives for Repeat Engagement ........................................................................................ 161

 C. Measuring and Optimising Loyalty Program Performance ........ 162

VIII. Building Advocacy and Word-of-Mouth Marketing .................. 163

 A. Encouraging User-Generated Content and Customer Reviews . 163

 B. Empowering Brand Advocates and Influencers ....................... 163

 C. Leveraging Referral Programs and Ambassadorship Initiatives . 163

IX. Measuring Long-Term Relationship Success ................................ 164

 A. Key Performance Indicators (KPIs) for Relationship Building .... 164

 B. Analytics Tools and Metrics for Tracking Customer Engagement ........................................................................................ 165

 C. Continuous Optimisation Based on Relationship Insights ......... 165

X. Case Studies and Real-World Examples ......................................... 166

 A. Successful Long-Term Relationship Building Strategies in Action .................................................................................................. 166

 B. Lessons Learned and Best Practices from Industry Leaders ...... 166

XI. Challenges and Considerations in Relationship Building ............... 167

 A. Balancing Personalisation with Privacy and Data Protection ..... 167

 B. Overcoming Customer Engagement Fatigue and Burnout ........ 168

C. Addressing Cultural and Market Differences in Relationship Dynamics ................................................................................................. 168

XII. Future Trends and Opportunities in Relationship Building .......... 169

A. Emerging Technologies and Innovations Shaping Relationship Marketing ................................................................................................ 169

B. The Evolution of Customer Experience and Relationship Management ........................................................................................... 169

C. Strategies for Sustaining Long-Term Relationships in a Dynamic Landscape ................................................................................ 170

**Chapter 9: Adapting to Emerging Trends ............................................ 172**

I. Introduction to Emerging Trends in Content Marketing ................ 172

A. Understanding the Dynamic Nature of the Digital Landscape ... 172

B. Importance of Adaptation and Innovation in Content Marketing ................................................................................................ 172

C. Overview of Emerging Trends and Their Impact on Audience Engagement ........................................................................................... 173

II. Content Formats and Consumption Trends ................................... 173

A. Rise of Short-Form Video Content and Micro-Content .............. 173

B. Growth of Interactive and Immersive Content Experiences ...... 174

C. Evolution of Voice Search and Audio Content Consumption ..... 174

III. Platform and Channel Shifts ........................................................... 175

A. Emergence of New Social Media Platforms and Trends ............ 175

B. Shift Towards Visual-First Platforms and Visual Storytelling ..... 176

C. Increasing Importance of Niche and Community-Based Platforms ................................................................................................ 176

IV. Technology and Innovation in Content Creation ........................... 177

A. Role of Artificial Intelligence (AI) in Content Creation and Personalisation ...................................................................................... 177

B. Leveraging Augmented Reality (AR) and Virtual Reality (VR) Experiences ............................................................................................ 178

    C. Impact of Emerging Technologies on Content Distribution and Consumption ................................................................................178

  V. Data Privacy and Ethical Considerations .........................................179

    A. Growing Concerns Around Data Privacy and Protection ...........179

    B. Implementing Ethical Content Marketing Practices ...................180

    C. Balancing Personalisation with Privacy and Transparency ........180

  VI. Cultural and Societal Shifts ...........................................................181

    A. Addressing Diversity, Equity, and Inclusion in Content Marketing ................................................................................................181

    B. Reflecting Cultural Sensitivity and Responsiveness in Content Creation ..................................................................................................182

    C. Navigating Sensitive Topics and Social Issues in Content Strategy ...................................................................................................182

  VII. Sustainability and Corporate Social Responsibility (CSR) .............183

    A. Incorporating Sustainability Messaging and Practices in Content Marketing .................................................................................183

    B. Communicating CSR Initiatives and Social Impact Efforts ..........184

    C. Aligning Brand Values with Environmental and Social Responsibility ..........................................................................................184

  VIII. Future-Proofing Your Content Marketing Strategy .....................185

    A. Staying Agile and Adaptive in a Rapidly Changing Landscape ...185

    B. Investing in Continuous Learning and Innovation ......................186

    C. Strategies for Anticipating and Responding to Future Trends ...186

  IX. Case Studies and Examples of Successful Adaptation ...................187

    A. Organisations Embracing Emerging Trends and Innovations ....187

    B. Lessons Learned and Best Practices from Early Adopters ..........188

    C. Strategies for Embracing Change and Thriving in the Future ....188

  X. Challenges and Opportunities in Adapting to Emerging Trends ....189

    A. Overcoming Resistance to Change and Legacy Systems ............189

B. Seizing Opportunities for Growth and Innovation .....................190

C. Anticipating and Mitigating Risks Associated with Emerging Trends.................................................................................................190

XI. Conclusion: Embracing a Future-Forward Mindset.......................191

A. Recap of Key Insights and Strategies for Adapting to Emerging Trends.................................................................................................191

B. Encouragement for Embracing Change and Innovation in Content Marketing ..............................................................................192

C. Looking Ahead to a Future-Ready Content Strategy..................192

## Chapter 10: Conclusion ..............................................................194

I. Recap of Key Insights and Strategies.................................................194

A. Summary of Key Concepts and Takeaways..................................194

B. Review of Effective Content Marketing Strategies Explored Throughout the Book ..........................................................................194

C. The Importance of Audience Engagement in Content Marketing Success..............................................................................195

II. Reflection on the Evolution of Content Marketing ........................196

A. Overview of How Content Marketing Has Evolved Over Time ..196

B. Emerging Trends and Future Directions in Content Marketing .196

C. Reflection on the Dynamic Nature of the Digital Landscape .....198

III. Encouragement for Continued Growth and Innovation ...............199

A. Embracing a Culture of Continuous Learning and Adaptation...199

B. Importance of Experimentation and Iterative Optimisation......200

C. Motivation to Stay Ahead of the Curve and Embrace Change...200

IV. Call to Action for Implementing Strategies....................................200

A. Empowering Readers to Apply Strategies and Tactics Discussed in the Book..........................................................................201

B. Encouragement for Taking Action and Implementing Content Marketing Initiatives ............................................................................202

C. Resources and Support for Your Content Marketing Journey ...203

V. Acknowledgment and Gratitude ....................................................204

A. Thanking Contributors, Mentors, and Inspirations ....................204

B. Expressing Gratitude for the Opportunity to Share Knowledge and Insights ...............................................................................................205

VII. Conclusion: Empowering Readers to Make an Impact ................205

A. Final Thoughts and Words of Encouragement..........................206

B. In Summary ...............................................................................206

**Glossary**.........................................................................................**207**

**Index** ..................................................................................................**1**

Engage & Convert

# Chapter 1: Introduction

## I. The Importance of Audience Engagement in Content Marketing

In the bustling world of digital marketing, where attention is the ultimate currency, mastering the art of audience engagement is paramount. Welcome to "Engage & Convert: Advanced Content Marketing Techniques." In this comprehensive guide, we embark on a journey through the intricate landscape of content marketing, unveiling the strategies and tactics essential for captivating audiences in today's dynamic digital ecosystem.

As traditional advertising methods lose their efficacy in the face of ad blockers and consumer scepticism, content marketing emerges as a beacon of authenticity and value. At its core lies the concept of audience engagement—a multifaceted phenomenon that transcends mere likes and shares. Audience engagement is the pulse that measures the vitality of your content, reflecting the depth of connection between brands and their audiences.

This book is crafted for marketing professionals, business owners, and content creators seeking to navigate the ever-changing currents of digital marketing with finesse. Whether you're a seasoned marketer looking to refine your strategies or a newcomer eager to make a splash in the digital sphere, the insights and techniques presented here will empower you to forge meaningful connections with your target audience.

Join us as we unravel the secrets to crafting compelling content, leveraging distribution channels, fostering community engagement, and nurturing long-term relationships with your audience. Together, let's embark on a transformative journey to unlock the full potential of content marketing and propel your brand to new heights of success.

### A. Defining Audience Engagement and Its Significance

Audience engagement encompasses the myriad of ways in which individuals interact with and respond to content, ranging from likes, comments, and shares to deeper forms of involvement such as active participation and brand advocacy. It transcends mere metrics, serving as a barometer of audience interest, sentiment, and connection with a brand or content creator. Significantly, audience engagement fosters a two-way dialogue, transforming passive consumers into active participants in the brand's narrative. In today's digital landscape, where consumer attention is fragmented and fleeting, cultivating meaningful audience engagement is essential for brands to cut through the noise, build trust, and foster long-lasting relationships with their target audience.

## B. The Shift from Traditional Marketing to Content Marketing

In the annals of marketing history, the rise of content marketing marks a seismic shift in how brands engage with their audience. Traditional marketing, characterised by interruptive advertising tactics, often struggled to capture and retain consumer attention in an increasingly cluttered media landscape. Television commercials, print ads, and billboards, while effective in their heyday, faced mounting challenges in an era dominated by ad blockers, DVRs, and declining print readership.

Enter content marketing—a paradigm shift that places value creation and audience engagement at its core. Unlike traditional marketing, which relies on intrusive messages to interrupt the consumer's experience, content marketing seeks to provide genuine value to the audience through relevant, informative, and entertaining content. By aligning with the audience's interests, needs, and preferences, brands can forge deeper connections and foster trust with their target demographic.

The digital revolution has played a pivotal role in catalysing the ascent of content marketing. The proliferation of digital channels, social media platforms, and mobile devices has empowered consumers with unprecedented control over their media consumption. In this democratised media landscape, consumers gravitate towards content that resonates with their passions, addresses their pain points, or entertains them in meaningful ways.

Moreover, the advent of digital analytics has enabled marketers to track and measure audience engagement with unparalleled precision. Metrics such as likes, shares, comments, and time spent on page provide valuable insights into audience preferences and behaviours, allowing brands to refine their content strategies in real-time.

In essence, the shift from traditional marketing to content marketing represents a fundamental reorientation from broadcasting messages to building relationships. By embracing the principles of content marketing, brands can transcend the limitations of traditional advertising and forge genuine connections with their audience, laying the foundation for long-term success in the digital age.

## C. Why Audience Engagement Matters More Than Ever

In the fast-paced landscape of modern marketing, audience engagement emerges as the linchpin of success, wielding greater significance than ever before. As consumers become increasingly discerning and empowered, brands must adapt their strategies to capture and maintain attention in a sea of competing messages. Here's why audience engagement stands as the cornerstone of effective marketing in the digital age:

a) Attention is the Currency: In an era characterised by information overload and fleeting consumer attention spans, capturing and retaining audience attention is akin to currency. With countless options vying for their attention, consumers gravitate towards content that resonates with their interests, entertains them, or provides genuine value. Brands that fail to engage their audience risk being relegated to the side-lines, overshadowed by competitors who understand the importance of captivating content.

b) Building Trust and Loyalty: Audience engagement serves as a vehicle for building trust and fostering loyalty among consumers. When brands consistently deliver valuable and relevant content, they demonstrate their commitment to meeting the needs and interests of their audience. Over time, this fosters a sense of trust and loyalty, transforming casual consumers into brand advocates who are more likely to recommend, advocate for, and remain loyal to the brand.

c) Amplifying Reach and Impact: Engaged audiences are not passive bystanders but active participants in the brand's narrative. When individuals engage with content by liking, sharing, or commenting, they amplify its reach and impact, extending its influence far beyond its initial audience. By nurturing engagement, brands can harness the power of word-of-mouth marketing and user-generated content, leveraging their audience as ambassadors to amplify their message.

d) Driving Conversions and Revenue: Ultimately, the goal of marketing is to drive meaningful outcomes, whether it's generating leads, increasing sales, or cultivating brand affinity. Audience engagement plays a pivotal role in this process by guiding consumers through the marketing funnel and nudging them towards conversion. Engaged audiences are more receptive to marketing messages, more likely to explore product offerings, and more inclined to make purchasing decisions, thereby driving revenue and ROI for the brand.

e) Adapting to Evolving Consumer Preferences: In a landscape characterised by rapid technological advancements and shifting consumer behaviours, audience engagement serves as a barometer of relevance and resonance. By monitoring audience engagement metrics, brands can gain valuable insights into changing consumer preferences, emerging trends, and areas of opportunity. This enables them to adapt their strategies in real-time, ensuring continued relevance and effectiveness in a constantly evolving marketplace.

In essence, audience engagement is not merely a metric to be measured but a strategic imperative that underpins the success of modern marketing efforts. By prioritising audience engagement and investing in strategies that resonate with their target demographic, brands can forge deeper connections, drive meaningful outcomes, and thrive in an increasingly competitive landscape.

## II. Setting the Stage: The Landscape of Content Marketing

### A. Evolution of Content Marketing: From Print to Digital

Content marketing has undergone a transformative journey from its inception in the print era to its current digital prominence, reshaping how brands connect with their audiences.

#### *1. Print Era: Seeds of Content Marketing*

The roots of content marketing can be traced back to the early days of print media, where brands utilised newspapers, magazines, and other printed materials to disseminate promotional content. Advertisements were seamlessly integrated into editorial content, blurring the lines between advertising and information. Brands sought to engage audiences by providing valuable and relevant content alongside their marketing messages, laying the groundwork for the future evolution of content marketing strategies.

#### *2. Broadcasting Age: Television and Radio*

The advent of television and radio brought about a new era of broadcasting, enabling brands to reach mass audiences with audio-visual content. Commercials, sponsored programs, and product placements became staple features of television and radio broadcasts, allowing brands to captivate audiences on a grand scale. While broadcasting provided unprecedented reach, it lacked the targeted and interactive capabilities that define modern content marketing approaches.

#### *3. Digital Revolution: Birth of Content Marketing*

The emergence of the internet and digital technologies marked a pivotal moment in the evolution of content marketing. With the rise of websites, blogs, and social media platforms, brands gained new avenues for engaging with their audiences directly. Content marketing shifted from traditional advertising methods to a more nuanced approach focused on creating valuable and relevant content that resonated with consumers. Brands began leveraging digital channels to publish articles, videos, and multimedia content, aiming to educate, entertain, and inspire their target demographic.

*4. Rise of User-Generated Content and social media*

The proliferation of social media platforms further accelerated the evolution of content marketing, empowering consumers to become active participants in brand storytelling. User-generated content, such as reviews, testimonials, and social media posts, became powerful tools for building credibility and trust. Brands embraced social media as a means of fostering community engagement, encouraging conversations, and eliciting user-generated content from their audience. Social media platforms provided brands with unprecedented access to real-time feedback and insights, enabling them to refine their content strategies based on audience preferences and behaviours.

*5. Continual Innovation: Interactive and Immersive Experiences*

In the digital age, content marketing continues to evolve, with brands exploring innovative formats to captivate audiences in new and engaging ways. From interactive quizzes and augmented reality experiences to immersive video content and virtual reality simulations, brands are leveraging cutting-edge technologies to create memorable brand experiences. This shift towards interactive and immersive content reflects a broader trend towards experiential marketing strategies that prioritise engagement and authenticity.

In summary, the evolution of content marketing from print to digital represents a journey marked by innovation, adaptation, and a relentless focus on engaging audiences in meaningful ways. As technology continues to advance and consumer behaviours evolve, content marketing will continue to evolve alongside them, shaping the future of brand-consumer relationships.

## B. Current Trends and Challenges in Content Marketing

As content marketing continues to evolve, it is imperative for marketers to stay abreast of current trends and navigate the challenges that accompany this dynamic landscape.

*1. Trends Shaping Content Marketing*

a) Video Dominance: Video content has emerged as a dominant force in content marketing, with platforms like YouTube, TikTok, and Instagram leading the charge. Brands are investing in high-quality video production to engage audiences through storytelling, tutorials, behind-the-scenes glimpses, and immersive experiences.

b) User-Generated Content: User-generated content (UGC) has gained traction as a powerful tool for building authenticity and trust. Brands are leveraging UGC in their marketing campaigns, tapping into the creativity and advocacy of their audience to amplify their brand message.

c) Personalisation and AI: Personalised content experiences are becoming increasingly prevalent, driven by advancements in artificial intelligence (AI) and machine learning. Brands are leveraging data-driven insights to deliver tailored content recommendations, emails, and advertisements that resonate with individual preferences and behaviours.

d) Interactive Content Formats: Interactive content formats, such as quizzes, polls, assessments, and interactive videos, are gaining popularity for their ability to engage audiences and drive meaningful interactions. Brands are incorporating interactive elements into their content strategies to increase engagement and capture valuable data insights.

*2. Challenges Facing Content Marketers*

a) Content Overload: The proliferation of content across digital channels has led to content overload, making it challenging for brands to stand out amidst the noise. Marketers must strive to create high-quality, differentiated content that cuts through the clutter and resonates with their target audience.

b) Algorithm Changes: Algorithm changes on social media platforms and search engines can significantly impact organic reach and visibility. Marketers must stay informed about algorithm updates and adapt their strategies accordingly to maintain engagement and reach.

c) Measurement and ROI: Measuring the effectiveness of content marketing initiatives and demonstrating ROI remains a persistent challenge for many marketers. Determining the impact of content on key performance indicators (KPIs) such as brand awareness, engagement, and conversion requires robust analytics and attribution models.

d) Content Distribution: Effectively distributing content to the right audience at the right time poses a challenge for marketers. With fragmented audience segments and diverse digital channels, marketers must develop targeted distribution strategies to maximise reach and engagement.

In summary, staying abreast of current trends and navigating the challenges in content marketing is essential for marketers looking to drive meaningful results and stay competitive in today's digital landscape. By embracing emerging trends and addressing key challenges, marketers can unlock the full potential of content marketing to engage audiences and achieve business objectives.

C. Opportunities for Brands in Engaging Audiences Through Content

In the dynamic landscape of content marketing, brands have abundant opportunities to connect with their audiences in meaningful ways, fostering engagement, building relationships, and driving business outcomes.

*1. Embracing Diverse Content Formats*

a) Visual Storytelling: With the rise of visual-centric platforms like Instagram, Snapchat, and Pinterest, brands can leverage the power of visual storytelling to engage audiences. Compelling visuals, such as images, infographics, and videos, can captivate audiences and convey brand messages in a memorable and impactful manner.

b) Interactive Content: Interactive content formats, such as quizzes, polls, interactive videos, and assessments, offer brands the opportunity to engage audiences in two-way conversations and drive active participation. By inviting audiences to interact with content, brands can deepen engagement and create immersive experiences that resonate with their target demographic.

c) Long-Form Content: While short-form content dominates many digital channels, long-form content presents an opportunity for brands to provide in-depth, comprehensive insights on complex topics. Blogs, whitepapers, e-books, and case studies offer brands a platform to showcase thought leadership, establish credibility, and engage audiences with valuable information.

*2. Leveraging Emerging Technologies*

a) Augmented Reality (AR) and Virtual Reality (VR): AR and VR technologies offer brands the opportunity to create immersive, interactive experiences that blur the lines between the physical and digital worlds. Brands can leverage AR and VR to showcase products, simulate real-world scenarios, and engage audiences in unique and memorable ways.

b) Voice Search and AI Assistants: The rise of voice search and AI-powered virtual assistants presents brands with new opportunities to engage audiences through conversational interactions. Brands can optimise content for voice search queries, develop voice-activated applications, and leverage AI assistants to provide personalised recommendations and assistance to users.

*3. Cultivating Community Engagement*

a) Brand Communities: Brands can foster community engagement by creating and nurturing online communities where customers can connect, share experiences, and interact with one another. By providing a platform for community engagement, brands can build loyalty, facilitate peer-to-peer support, and harness the collective wisdom of their audience.

b) User-Generated Content (UGC): Encouraging user-generated content, such as reviews, testimonials, and user-submitted photos or videos, empowers customers to become brand advocates and ambassadors. UGC not only builds authenticity and trust but also provides brands with valuable social proof and organic word-of-mouth marketing.

*4. Data-Driven Personalisation*

a) Personalised Recommendations: Leveraging data analytics and machine learning algorithms, brands can deliver personalised content recommendations tailored to individual preferences and behaviours. By serving relevant content to each user, brands can enhance engagement, increase dwell time, and drive conversions.

b) Dynamic Content: Dynamic content allows brands to create personalised experiences by dynamically adapting content based on user attributes, preferences, and contextual factors. Whether through personalised emails, website content, or advertisements, dynamic content enables brands to deliver targeted messages that resonate with everyone.

In summary, the opportunities for brands to engage audiences through content are vast and diverse. By embracing diverse content formats, leveraging emerging technologies, cultivating community engagement, and embracing data-driven personalisation, brands can create meaningful experiences that resonate with their audiences, drive engagement, and achieve business objectives.

## III. Objectives and Structure of the Book

### A. Overview of the Book's Purpose and Goals

"Engage & Convert: Advanced Content Marketing Techniques" is crafted with the intention of serving as a guiding light for marketers, business owners, and content creators seeking to excel in the realm of content marketing. This section offers a comprehensive overview of the book's overarching purpose and the goals it aims to achieve.

*Understanding Audience Engagement*

The primary objective of this book is to provide readers with a deep understanding of audience engagement and its pivotal role in content marketing. By elucidating the significance of audience engagement and its impact on brand-consumer relationships, readers gain essential insights into why engaging audiences is paramount for achieving marketing objectives.

*Exploring Effective Content Marketing Strategies*

Throughout the chapters, we delve into a diverse array of content marketing strategies meticulously designed to captivate audiences and foster meaningful connections. From crafting compelling content to optimising distribution channels and fostering community engagement, readers will be equipped with a comprehensive toolkit of strategies tailored to engage audiences across various platforms and mediums.

*Embracing Evolving Trends and Technologies*

In addition to exploring established content marketing strategies, this book endeavours to shed light on emerging trends and technologies shaping the future of audience engagement. By examining innovative approaches such as interactive content formats, AI-driven personalisation, and immersive experiences, readers gain insights into how they can leverage cutting-edge innovations to stay ahead of the curve and drive engagement in an ever-evolving digital landscape.

*Practical Implementation and Measurement*

Practical implementation and measurement lie at the heart of this book's objectives. By providing actionable steps, techniques, and measurement frameworks, readers are empowered to translate theoretical insights into tangible results. From developing audience personas to analysing engagement metrics and refining content strategies, readers will acquire the tools and methodologies necessary to measure the impact of their efforts effectively and drive continuous improvement.

*Empowering Readers for Success*

Ultimately, the overarching goal of "Engage & Convert: Advanced Content Marketing Techniques" is to empower readers with the knowledge, skills, and confidence needed to succeed in content marketing. Whether readers are seasoned marketers seeking to refine their strategies or newcomers eager to make a mark in the digital sphere, this book offers invaluable insights and guidance to help them navigate the ever-changing landscape of content marketing and drive meaningful results for their brands.

B. Explanation of the Book's Organisation and Flow

Understanding the organisation and flow of "Engage & Convert: Advanced Content Marketing Techniques" is crucial for readers to navigate through its contents effectively. This section provides an overview of how the book is structured and the logical progression of chapters.

a) Sequential Progression: The book follows a logical sequence, beginning with foundational concepts before gradually delving into more advanced topics. Each chapter builds upon the knowledge and insights presented in the preceding chapters, ensuring a smooth and cohesive learning experience for readers.

b) Foundational Concepts: The initial chapters lay the groundwork by introducing fundamental concepts such as audience engagement, content creation, and distribution channels. Readers gain a solid understanding of the core principles that underpin effective content marketing strategies.

c) In-Depth Exploration: Subsequent chapters dive deeper into specific aspects of content marketing, exploring topics such as community engagement, personalisation, and measurement and analytics. Each chapter provides in-depth insights, practical tips, and real-world examples to illustrate key concepts and strategies.

d) Practical Application: Throughout the book, readers are encouraged to apply the concepts and strategies discussed to their own marketing endeavours. Actionable advice and step-by-step guidance enable readers to implement what they've learned and achieve tangible results in their content marketing efforts.

e) Integration of Case Studies and Examples: The book integrates case studies and examples from various industries to illustrate how different organisations have successfully implemented content marketing strategies to engage their audiences. These real-world examples provide inspiration and practical insights for readers seeking to apply similar strategies in their own contexts.

f) Summarisation and Reflection: Each chapter concludes with a summary of key takeaways and reflection questions to help readers consolidate their understanding and apply the concepts to their own situations. This reflective approach fosters deeper learning and encourages readers to think critically about how they can leverage content marketing strategies to achieve their goals.

By providing a clear explanation of the book's organisation and flow, readers can navigate through "Engage & Convert: Advanced Content Marketing Techniques" with confidence, extracting valuable insights and practical strategies to enhance their content marketing efforts and drive meaningful results for their brands.

## C. What Readers Can Expect to Gain from Each Chapter

Understanding the specific insights and skills readers can expect to gain from each chapter is essential for maximising the value of "Engage & Convert: Advanced Content Marketing Techniques." This section outlines the key benefits readers can anticipate from each chapter.

a) Introduction:

Readers will gain an understanding of the evolution of content marketing and the importance of audience engagement in modern marketing practices. They will also receive an overview of the book's objectives and structure, setting the stage for what lies ahead.

b) Understanding Your Audience:

Readers will learn how to define their target audience, conduct audience research, and create detailed audience personas. By understanding their audience's preferences, behaviours, and demographics, readers can tailor their content to resonate with their target demographic effectively.

c) Crafting Compelling Content:

This chapter equips readers with the skills and techniques necessary to create compelling content that captivates audiences. From storytelling principles to the creation of visual and interactive content, readers will learn how to craft content that resonates with their audience and drives engagement.

d) Leveraging Distribution Channels:

Readers will explore various distribution channels, including social media, email marketing, and search engine optimisation (SEO). By understanding how to leverage these channels effectively, readers can maximise the reach and visibility of their content and connect with their audience across multiple touchpoints.

e) Building Community Engagement:

This chapter focuses on strategies for building and nurturing online communities around a brand or content. Readers will learn how to foster user-generated content, collaborate with influencers, and create a sense of belonging among their audience, leading to increased engagement and brand loyalty.

f) Measuring Engagement and Analytics:

Readers will discover key metrics for measuring audience engagement and how to use analytics tools to track and analyse engagement data. By interpreting data insights, readers can identify areas for improvement and optimise their content marketing strategies for maximum impact.

g) Enhancing Engagement through Personalisation:

This chapter explores the importance of personalisation in content marketing and how to implement personalised content strategies effectively. Readers will learn how to customise content for different audience segments, leverage AI and machine learning for personalisation, and deliver dynamic content experiences.

h) Nurturing Long-Term Relationships:

Readers will gain insights into strategies for building trust, fostering brand loyalty, and turning engaged audiences into brand advocates. By nurturing long-term relationships with their audience, readers can cultivate a loyal customer base and drive sustained business growth.

i) Adapting to Emerging Trends:

This chapter examines emerging trends and technologies shaping the future of content marketing. Readers will explore innovative strategies such as voice search, interactive content, and AI-driven personalisation, and learn how to adapt their marketing efforts to stay ahead of the curve.

j) Conclusion:

In the final chapter, readers will receive a recap of key strategies and insights from the book. They will also gain a glimpse into the future of audience engagement in content marketing and receive actionable takeaways to apply in their own marketing endeavours.

## IV. Who This Book Is For

### A. Target Audience: Marketing Professionals, Business Owners, and Content Creators

"Engage & Convert: Advanced Content Marketing Techniques" is tailored to meet the needs of a diverse audience comprising marketing professionals, business owners, and content creators who are seeking to excel in content marketing and audience engagement. This section highlights the relevance of the book for each of these key audience segments.

a)  Marketing Professionals:

Marketing professionals, including digital marketers, brand managers, and marketing executives, will find this book invaluable for enhancing their skills and knowledge in content marketing. Whether they are looking to refine their existing strategies or explore innovative approaches, this book provides practical insights and strategies to help them drive engagement and achieve their marketing objectives.

b)  Business Owners:

Business owners and entrepreneurs who are responsible for overseeing their company's marketing efforts will benefit from the practical guidance offered in this book. By understanding the principles of audience engagement and content marketing, business owners can make informed decisions about their marketing strategies, allocate resources effectively, and drive growth for their business.

c)  Content Creators:

Content creators, including writers, designers, videographers, and social media managers, play a crucial role in executing content marketing strategies. This book equips content creators with the skills and techniques necessary to create compelling content that resonates with their target audience. From storytelling principles to content optimisation strategies, content creators will find actionable insights to enhance the effectiveness of their content.

d)  Aspiring Professionals:

Additionally, aspiring marketing professionals and individuals looking to enter the field of content marketing will find this book to be a valuable resource for building foundational knowledge and skills. By learning from real-world examples and case studies, aspiring professionals can gain a deeper understanding of content marketing principles and best practices, positioning themselves for success in their careers.

In summary, "Engage & Convert: Advanced Content Marketing Techniques" caters to a broad audience encompassing marketing professionals, business owners, content creators, and aspiring professionals alike. By providing practical insights, actionable strategies, and real-world examples, this book empowers readers to excel in content marketing and drive meaningful results for their brands and businesses.

B. How This Book Can Benefit Readers in Different Roles and Industries

"Engage & Convert: Advanced Content Marketing Techniques" offers valuable insights and practical strategies that cater to the diverse needs of readers across various roles and industries. This section highlights the specific benefits that readers can expect based on their roles and industries.

a) Marketing Professionals:

Marketing professionals, including digital marketers, brand managers, and marketing executives, will benefit from the comprehensive coverage of content marketing strategies and tactics. They will gain insights into audience engagement, content creation, distribution channels, and measurement techniques, enabling them to optimise their marketing efforts and drive results for their organisations.

b) Business Owners and Entrepreneurs:

Business owners and entrepreneurs can leverage the strategies outlined in this book to enhance their company's marketing initiatives. By understanding the principles of content marketing and audience engagement, business owners can make informed decisions about their marketing strategies, allocate resources effectively, and drive growth for their businesses.

c) Content Creators:

Content creators, including writers, designers, videographers, and social media managers, will find practical guidance and actionable tips to enhance the effectiveness of their content. Whether they are creating blog posts, videos, social media content, or email campaigns, content creators will learn how to craft compelling content that resonates with their target audience and drives engagement.

d) Industry Professionals:

Professionals working in specific industries, such as healthcare, technology, finance, and retail, can apply the principles of content marketing outlined in this book to their respective fields. By understanding their audience's preferences and pain points, industry professionals can create tailored content that addresses their specific needs and positions their brand as a trusted authority in their industry.

e) Aspiring Professionals and Students:

Aspiring professionals and students looking to enter the field of marketing will find this book to be a valuable resource for building foundational knowledge and skills. By learning from real-world examples and case studies, aspiring professionals can gain a deeper understanding of content marketing principles and best practices, preparing themselves for successful careers in the field.

In summary, "Engage & Convert: Advanced Content Marketing Techniques" caters to readers across various roles and industries, offering practical insights and actionable strategies to help them excel in content marketing. Whether readers are marketing professionals, business owners, content creators, or aspiring professionals, this book provides the tools and knowledge they need to drive engagement and achieve their marketing objectives effectively.

## C. Why Audience Engagement Is Relevant Across Various Sectors

Audience engagement holds profound relevance across diverse sectors and industries, transcending boundaries and impacting organisations of all types. This section elucidates why audience engagement is a critical consideration across various sectors, underscoring its universal importance.

a) Healthcare Industry:

In the healthcare sector, audience engagement plays a crucial role in patient education, disease management, and healthcare promotion. By creating informative and engaging content, healthcare organisations can empower patients to take control of their health, increase compliance with treatment plans, and foster healthier behaviours.

b) Technology Sector:

In the technology sector, audience engagement is essential for building brand awareness, driving product adoption, and fostering customer loyalty. By creating compelling content that highlights the value proposition of their products and services, technology companies can attract and retain customers in an increasingly competitive market.

c) Finance and Banking:

In the finance and banking industry, audience engagement is vital for building trust, providing financial education, and driving customer acquisition. By delivering personalised and relevant content, financial institutions can enhance their reputation, deepen customer relationships, and increase customer lifetime value.

d) Retail and E-commerce:

In the retail and e-commerce sector, audience engagement is instrumental in driving sales, increasing customer retention, and fostering brand advocacy. By creating immersive and interactive shopping experiences, retailers can captivate audiences, encourage repeat purchases, and leverage user-generated content to showcase products and enhance social proof.

e) Education and Non-profit Organisations:

In the education and non-profit sectors, audience engagement is essential for raising awareness, mobilising support, and driving social change. By creating compelling narratives and leveraging storytelling techniques, educational institutions and non-profits can inspire action, cultivate donor relationships, and amplify their impact in the community.

f) Professional Services:

In professional services industries such as legal, consulting, and accounting, audience engagement is critical for building credibility, attracting clients, and driving business growth. By demonstrating expertise through thought leadership content, professional services firms can differentiate themselves in a crowded marketplace and attract high-value clients.

In summary, audience engagement is relevant across various sectors and industries due to its profound impact on brand perception, customer relationships, and business outcomes. By prioritising audience engagement and creating compelling content that resonates with their target audience, organisations can drive meaningful results and achieve their strategic objectives effectively, regardless of their sector or industry.

## V. How to Use This Book

## A. Guide to Navigating Through Chapters and Sections

Navigating through the chapters and sections of "Engage & Convert: Advanced Content Marketing Techniques" is designed to be intuitive and user-friendly, providing readers with a seamless reading experience. This guide offers practical tips for efficiently navigating through the book's contents.

a) Table of Contents:

The table of contents provides a comprehensive overview of the book's structure, outlining the chapters and sections in sequential order. Readers can use the table of contents to quickly locate specific topics of interest and navigate to relevant sections with ease.

b) Chapter Introductions:

Each chapter begins with a concise introduction that highlights the key themes, objectives, and takeaways covered in the chapter. By reading the chapter introductions, readers can gain a clear understanding of what to expect and how each chapter contributes to the overall narrative of the book.

c) Subheadings and Section Summaries:

Within each chapter, subheadings and section summaries are provided to help readers navigate through the content and identify key concepts and insights. Subheadings delineate different topics within the chapter, while section summaries offer brief recaps of the main points covered in each section.

d) Cross-References:

Throughout the book, cross-references are included to connect related topics and direct readers to additional resources or relevant sections within the book. By following cross-references, readers can explore interconnected concepts and deepen their understanding of specific topics.

e) Index and Glossary:

The book features an index and glossary at the end, providing readers with a reference guide to key terms and concepts discussed throughout the book. The index allows readers to quickly locate specific terms or topics, while the glossary offers concise definitions and explanations for clarity.

f) Actionable Takeaways and Reflection Questions:
At the end of each chapter, actionable takeaways and reflection questions are provided to encourage readers to apply the concepts and insights discussed in their own contexts. By reflecting on the key takeaways and considering how to implement them in their own marketing endeavours, readers can maximise the value they derive from each chapter.

By leveraging these resources, readers can effectively navigate through the chapters and sections of "Engage & Convert: Advanced Content Marketing Techniques," gaining valuable insights and actionable strategies to enhance their content marketing efforts and drive meaningful results for their brands and businesses.

## B. Suggestions for Active Engagement and Application of Strategies

Engaging actively with the content and applying the strategies outlined in "Engage & Convert: Advanced Content Marketing Techniques" is essential for maximising learning and driving tangible results. This section provides practical suggestions for how readers can actively engage with the content and apply the strategies discussed in each chapter.

a) Interactive Exercises:

Throughout the book, readers will encounter interactive exercises designed to encourage active participation and facilitate learning. These exercises may include brainstorming sessions, content creation prompts, and audience engagement challenges aimed at applying the concepts discussed in real-world scenarios.

b) Case Studies and Examples:

Pay close attention to the case studies and examples provided in each chapter, as they offer valuable insights into how real-world organisations have successfully implemented content marketing strategies. Reflect on these case studies and consider how similar strategies could be applied to your own brand or business.

c) Actionable Takeaways:

At the end of each chapter, take note of the actionable takeaways and key points summarised. Consider how these takeaways can be applied to your specific context and develop an action plan for implementing them in your content marketing efforts.

d) Reflection and Application:

Take time to reflect on the concepts discussed in each chapter and consider how they relate to your own experiences and challenges. Identify specific areas where you can apply the strategies and techniques discussed and develop a plan for incorporating them into your content marketing strategy.

e) Experimentation and Iteration:

Embrace a mindset of experimentation and iteration as you implement new strategies and techniques. Be willing to test different approaches, measure the results, and iterate based on feedback and insights gained along the way. This iterative approach will help you refine your content marketing efforts and drive continuous improvement.

By actively engaging with the content and applying the strategies discussed in "Engage & Convert: Advanced Content Marketing Techniques," readers can maximise their learning experience and achieve meaningful results in their content marketing endeavours.

### C. Resources and Tools Recommended Throughout the Book

Throughout "Engage & Convert: Advanced Content Marketing Techniques," readers will encounter a variety of resources and tools recommended to enhance their understanding and implementation of content marketing strategies. This section highlights some of the key resources and tools recommended throughout the book.

a) Content Creation Tools:

Tools such as Canva, Adobe Creative Cloud, and Grammarly are recommended for creating visually appealing and well-written content. These tools offer features for designing graphics, editing images, and checking spelling and grammar, enhancing the quality and professionalism of your content.

b) Analytics Platforms:

Platforms such as Google Analytics, Adobe Analytics, and social media analytics tools are recommended for tracking and analysing audience engagement metrics. These tools provide valuable insights into website traffic, user behaviour, and content performance, enabling you to measure the effectiveness of your content marketing efforts.

c) Marketing Automation Software:

Marketing automation software such as HubSpot, Mailchimp, and Marketo are recommended for streamlining content distribution, email marketing, and lead nurturing processes.

These platforms offer features for scheduling content, segmenting audiences, and automating marketing workflows, saving time and increasing efficiency.

d) Content Collaboration Platforms:

Collaboration platforms such as Google Workspace, Microsoft Teams, and Slack are recommended for facilitating communication and collaboration among content marketing teams. These platforms provide tools for sharing documents, coordinating projects, and communicating in real-time, fostering collaboration and teamwork.

e) Educational Resources:

Educational resources such as online courses, webinars, and industry blogs are recommended for staying updated on the latest trends and best practices in content marketing. Platforms such as Coursera, Udemy, and Content Marketing Institute offer a wealth of educational resources for expanding your knowledge and skills in content marketing.

By leveraging these resources and tools recommended throughout the book, readers can enhance their understanding of content marketing strategies and optimise their implementation for maximum effectiveness.

## VI. Meet the Author

### A. Background and Expertise in Technology and the Digital World

The author has been immersed in the family advertising and marketing business from an early age, leveraging strong people skills to build a parallel career in Technology and Project Management. Drawing from these years of experience and expertise the author brings a wealth of knowledge to the table. With relevant backgrounds spanning digital marketing, brand management, and content creation, he has honed his skills over the years assisting in crafting compelling content, optimising distribution channels, and measuring audience engagement metrics. A deep understanding of audience psychology, consumer behaviour, and emerging trends in the digital landscape informs the strategies and insights shared in this book. Readers can trust in the credibility and authority of the author and contributors to provide practical guidance and actionable strategies for driving meaningful results in content marketing and audience engagement.

### B. Inspiration Behind Writing the Book

The inspiration behind writing "Engage & Convert: Advanced Content Marketing Techniques" stems from a shared passion for helping marketers, business owners, and content creators succeed in the ever-evolving landscape of content marketing. Recognising the importance of audience engagement as a cornerstone of effective marketing strategies, the author has sought to distil his knowledge and experiences into a comprehensive guide that empowers readers to navigate the complexities of content marketing with confidence. The author is driven by a desire to share actionable strategies, real-world examples, and practical insights that enable readers to unlock the full potential of content marketing and drive meaningful results for their brands and businesses. It is their hope that this book serves as a valuable resource and source of inspiration for readers seeking to excel in content marketing and audience engagement.

## VII. Conclusion

### A. Recap of Key Points Covered in the Introduction

In the introduction to "Engage & Convert: Advanced Content Marketing Techniques," we laid the foundation for our exploration of content marketing and audience engagement. Key points covered include:

a) Definition of audience engagement and its significance in content marketing.

b) Overview of the book's objectives and structure, outlining the chapters and sections to come.

c) Introduction to the authors' background and expertise in content marketing and audience engagement.

d) Inspiration behind writing the book, driven by a desire to empower readers with actionable strategies and insights.

e) By understanding these key points, readers gain a clear understanding of the purpose and scope of the book, setting the stage for the insights and strategies to come.

## B. Anticipation of What's to Come in the Subsequent Chapters

As we embark on this journey through "Engage & Convert: Advanced Content Marketing Techniques," we anticipate delving into a wealth of knowledge and practical strategies designed to empower readers in their content marketing endeavours. In the subsequent chapters, readers can expect to:

a) Gain insights into understanding their audience and crafting compelling content tailored to their preferences and interests.

b) Explore strategies for leveraging distribution channels effectively to reach and engage target audiences across various platforms.

c) Dive into topics such as community engagement, personalisation, and measurement and analytics to drive meaningful results.

d) Discover emerging trends and technologies shaping the future of content marketing and audience engagement.

e) Each chapter will offer actionable insights, real-world examples where applicable, and practical tips to help readers navigate the complexities of content marketing and drive engagement with their target audiences.

C. Encouragement for Readers to Dive into the Content and Begin Their Journey Toward Mastering Content Marketing Strategies for Engaging Audiences.

With the groundwork laid and the path forward illuminated, we encourage readers to dive into the content and begin their journey toward mastering Engage & Convert: Advanced Content Marketing Techniques. Whether you're a seasoned marketer looking to refine your strategies or a newcomer eager to make a mark in the digital sphere, this book offers valuable insights and guidance to help you achieve your goals. By actively engaging with the content, applying the strategies discussed, and embracing a mindset of continuous learning and experimentation, you can unlock the full potential of content marketing and drive meaningful results for your brand or business. Your journey starts here—let's embark on it together.

# Chapter 2: Understanding Your Audience

## I. Introduction to Understanding Your Audience

In the dynamic landscape of content marketing, success hinges on one fundamental principle: understanding your audience. Welcome to the chapter on "Understanding Your Audience". This chapter serves as a compass, guiding you through the intricate terrain of audience analysis and insights. By unravelling the mysteries of your audience's preferences, behaviours, and needs, you can chart a course towards creating content that resonates deeply and fosters meaningful connections. Let's embark on this journey of discovery and unlock the secrets to audience engagement and loyalty.

### A. Importance of Audience Understanding in Content Marketing

Audience understanding lies at the heart of effective content marketing. In an era of information overload and shrinking attention spans, capturing and retaining audience interest is paramount. By understanding your audience intimately, you can tailor your content to meet their specific needs, preferences, and pain points. Audience understanding enables you to create content that is relevant, valuable, and compelling, leading to higher engagement, conversion rates, and brand loyalty. Moreover, audience insights serve as a guiding light, informing content strategy decisions and ensuring that your efforts are aligned with audience expectations and interests. In essence, audience understanding is the bedrock upon which successful content marketing strategies are built.

### B. Overview of Chapter Objectives and Structure

This chapter is structured to provide a comprehensive exploration of audience understanding in content marketing. We begin by examining the importance of audience understanding and its implications for content strategy. Next, we delve into the key objectives of the chapter, which include identifying target audience segments, creating audience personas, conducting audience research, and leveraging audience insights for content creation. Each section is designed to equip you with practical tools, techniques, and insights to deepen your understanding of your audience and enhance your content marketing efforts. By the end of this chapter, you will have the knowledge and skills necessary to unlock the full potential of audience understanding and drive meaningful results in your content marketing endeavours.

## II. Identifying Target Audience Segments

### A. Demographic Analysis

Demographic analysis involves examining key demographic factors of your audience to gain insights into their characteristics and preferences. By understanding demographic variables such as age, gender, location, income level, and education, you can segment your audience and tailor your content to resonate with specific demographic groups. Demographic analysis provides a foundational understanding of who your audience is and helps you identify trends and patterns that inform your content strategy.

### B. Psychographic Profiling

Psychographic profiling delves deeper into the psychological and lifestyle characteristics of your audience, uncovering their attitudes, values, interests, and behaviours. By understanding the psychographic profiles of your audience segments, you can develop a more nuanced understanding of their motivations, aspirations, and pain points. Psychographic profiling enables you to create content that resonates on an emotional level and connects with your audience's unique identities and lifestyles.

### C. Behavioural Segmentation

Behavioural segmentation involves analysing your audience's past behaviours and interactions to identify distinct segments based on their actions and preferences. By examining factors such as purchase history, browsing behaviour, engagement with content, and interaction with your brand, you can segment your audience according to their behavioural patterns. Behavioural segmentation provides insights into the actions and interests of your audience, allowing you to tailor content and messaging to meet their specific needs and interests.

### D. Customer Surveys and Feedback

Customer surveys and feedback offer direct insights into your audience's perceptions, preferences, and satisfaction levels. By soliciting feedback through surveys, polls, and reviews, you can gather valuable information about your audience's experiences, preferences, and areas for improvement. Customer feedback provides qualitative insights that complement quantitative data obtained through demographic analysis, psychographic profiling, and behavioural segmentation, offering a holistic understanding of your audience. Additionally, customer surveys and feedback foster engagement and interaction with your audience, strengthening relationships and building trust.

## III. Creating Audience Personas

### A. Definition and Purpose of Audience Personas

Audience personas are fictional representations of your ideal audience segments based on research and data analysis. These personas embody the demographic, psychographic, and behavioural characteristics of your target audience, allowing you to better understand their needs, preferences, and motivations. The purpose of audience personas is to humanise your target audience and provide a deeper understanding of their wants and pain points. By creating detailed personas, you can tailor your content and marketing strategies to effectively engage with different audience segments and deliver personalised experiences that resonate with their unique needs.

### B. Steps for Developing Audience Personas

Developing audience personas involves a systematic process of research, analysis, and synthesis to create accurate and representative representations of your target audience. The following steps can guide you through the process of developing audience personas:

   a) Conduct Audience Research: Gather data from sources such as surveys, interviews, and analytics to understand your audience's demographics, preferences, and behaviours.

   b) Identify Common Characteristics: Analyse the data to identify common patterns and characteristics among your audience segments, such as age, gender, interests, and pain points.

   c) Group Similar Traits: Group similar traits and behaviours to create distinct audience segments that represent different personas within your target audience.

   d) Create Persona Profiles: Develop detailed persona profiles for each audience segment, including demographic information, psychographic traits, goals, challenges, and preferred communication channels.

   e) Validate with Stakeholders: Validate the persona profiles with internal stakeholders, such as marketing teams, sales teams, and customer service representatives, to ensure accuracy and alignment with organisational goals.

## C. Examples of Effective Audience Personas

Effective audience personas are based on thorough research and accurately represent the characteristics and motivations of your target audience. Here are some examples of effective audience personas:

   a) Young Professionals: This persona represents young professionals in their 20s and 30s who are tech-savvy, ambitious, and career-oriented. They value convenience, flexibility, and personal development and are active on social media platforms.

b) Busy Parents: This persona represents busy parents with young children who are looking for time-saving solutions and family-friendly activities. They prioritise convenience, safety, and affordability and are interested in parenting tips, product reviews, and family-friendly events.

c) Retirees: This persona represents retirees who are enjoying their newfound freedom and are interested in travel, hobbies, and leisure activities. They value relaxation, adventure, and social connections and are active consumers of travel-related content, retirement planning advice, and lifestyle tips.

By creating detailed audience personas like these examples, you can gain a deeper understanding of your target audience and tailor your content and marketing strategies to effectively engage with them and meet their needs.

## IV. Conducting Audience Research

### A. Methods for Gathering Audience Data

Gathering audience data is crucial for understanding your audience's preferences, behaviours, and needs. Here are some methods for gathering audience data:

a) Surveys and Questionnaires: Conducting surveys and questionnaires allows you to collect quantitative and qualitative data directly from your audience. You can design surveys to gather information about demographics, interests, purchasing habits, and satisfaction levels.

b) Interviews and Focus Groups: Conducting interviews and focus groups provides an opportunity to delve deeper into your audience's motivations, pain points, and preferences. These qualitative research methods allow for open-ended discussions and rich insights into audience attitudes and behaviours.

c) Website and Social Media Analytics: Analysing website and social media analytics provides valuable data on audience demographics, engagement metrics, and content performance. Platforms like Google Analytics and social media insights tools offer insights into audience demographics, behaviour flow, and content engagement metrics.

d) Customer Feedback and Reviews: Monitoring customer feedback and reviews across various channels, such as social media, review websites, and customer service interactions, provides valuable insights into audience satisfaction levels, pain points, and preferences.

e) Market Research Reports and Studies: Leveraging market research reports and studies conducted by third-party research firms and industry organisations can provide valuable insights into broader market trends, consumer behaviours, and competitive landscapes.

## B. Analysing Audience Insights

Once you've gathered audience data, it's essential to analyse the insights to derive meaningful conclusions and actionable recommendations. Here are some steps for analysing audience insights:

a) Segmentation Analysis: Segment your audience data into distinct segments based on demographic, psychographic, and behavioural characteristics.

b) Pattern Recognition: Identify patterns and trends within each audience segment, such as common preferences and pain points.

c) Comparison and Benchmarking: Compare audience data across different segments and benchmark against industry averages or competitor data to identify areas of strength and areas for improvement.

d) Identifying Opportunities: Identify opportunities for content optimisation, product development, and marketing strategies based on audience insights and market trends.

e) Iterative Analysis: Continuously analyse audience insights over time to track changes in audience habits, preferences, and market dynamics, and adjust your strategies accordingly.

## C. Tools and Resources for Audience Research

Numerous tools and resources are available to facilitate audience research and analysis. Some of the key tools and resources for audience research include:

a) Google Analytics: A powerful web analytics tool that provides insights into website traffic, user behaviour, and audience demographics.

b) Social Media Insights: Platforms like Facebook Insights, Twitter Analytics, and Instagram Insights offer analytics dashboards with data on audience demographics, engagement metrics, and content performance.

c) Survey and Polling Platforms: Tools like SurveyMonkey, Google Forms, and Typeform enable you to create and distribute surveys and polls to gather audience feedback and insights.

d) Market Research Reports: Subscription-based market research platforms like Statista, IBISWorld, and Forrester Research provide access to comprehensive market research reports and studies on various industries and consumer trends.

e) Customer Relationship Management (CRM) Systems: CRM systems like Salesforce, HubSpot, and Zoho CRM store customer data and provide insights into customer interactions, purchase history, and communication preferences.

By leveraging these methods, tools, and resources for audience research and analysis, you can gain valuable insights into your audience's preferences and needs and inform your content marketing strategies effectively.

## V. Understanding Audience Needs and Preferences

### A. Identifying Pain Points and Challenges

Identifying pain points and challenges is the first step in creating content that resonates with your audience and provides valuable solutions. Pain points are specific problems, frustrations, or obstacles that your audience faces in their daily lives or in achieving their goals. By understanding these pain points, you can tailor your content to address the needs and concerns of your audience effectively.

To identify pain points and challenges, consider the following approaches:

a) Customer Feedback: Gather insights from customer feedback, reviews, and complaints to identify recurring themes or issues that customers are facing. Look for common frustrations or challenges mentioned by multiple customers.

b) Surveys and Interviews: Conduct surveys or interviews with your audience to gather first-hand insights into their pain points and challenges. Ask open-ended questions to encourage respondents to share their experiences and frustrations.

c) Social Listening: Monitor social media platforms, online forums, and review websites to listen to conversations about your brand, products, or industry. Look for trends or patterns in the discussions and identify common pain points or challenges mentioned by users.

d) Keyword Research: Use keyword research tools to identify search terms related to your industry or products that indicate potential pain points or challenges. Look for long-tail keywords that suggest specific problems or questions that users are seeking answers to.

Once you've identified your audience's pain points and challenges, prioritise them based on their severity, frequency, and relevance to your audience. Use this information to guide your content creation efforts and develop solutions-oriented content that addresses your audience's needs and resonates with their experiences.

## B. Assessing Content Preferences and Formats

Assessing your audience's content preferences and formats is essential for delivering content that resonates and engages with your audience effectively. Different audiences have varying preferences when it comes to content types, formats, and delivery channels. By understanding your audience's preferences, you can tailor your content to meet their expectations and preferences.

To assess your audience's content preferences and formats, consider the following approaches:

a) Content Consumption Habits: Analyse data from website analytics, social media insights, and email marketing metrics to understand how your audience consumes content. Look for trends in the types of content that receive the most engagement and interaction.

b) Audience Surveys and Feedback: Conduct surveys or gather feedback from your audience to understand their preferences for content types, formats, and topics. Ask questions about their preferred content formats (e.g., articles, videos, infographics), topics of interest, and preferred delivery channels.

c) Competitor Analysis: Analyse your competitors' content strategies to identify trends in content types, formats, and topics that resonate with your shared audience. Look for opportunities to differentiate your content while meeting your audience's preferences.

d) A/B Testing: Experiment with different content formats and delivery channels to assess their effectiveness in engaging with your audience. Use A/B testing to compare the performance of different content formats and optimise your content strategy accordingly.

By assessing your audience's content preferences and formats, you can tailor your content to meet their expectations and deliver a more engaging and personalised experience.

### C. Addressing Audience Needs Through Content Solutions

Once you've identified your audience's pain points and preferences, it's time to address their needs through content solutions. Content solutions are actionable and informative content pieces that provide value to your audience by addressing their specific challenges and offering practical solutions.

To address audience needs through content solutions, consider the following strategies:

a) Educational Content: Create educational content that helps your audience learn new skills, overcome challenges, or achieve their goals. This could include how-to guides, tutorials, or informative articles that provide practical advice and actionable tips.

b) Problem-Solving Content: Identify common pain points and challenges faced by your audience and develop content that offers solutions and strategies for overcoming them. This could include troubleshooting guides, problem-solving videos, or case studies that demonstrate real-world solutions.

c) Inspiration and Motivation: Create content that inspires and motivates your audience to act and pursue their goals. This could include success stories, inspirational quotes, or personal anecdotes that resonate with your audience's aspirations and values.

d) Interactive Content: Engage your audience with interactive content formats that encourage participation and engagement. This could include quizzes, polls, or interactive infographics that invite your audience to interact with your content and learn in a more dynamic way.

By addressing your audience's needs through content solutions, you can provide value, build trust, and strengthen relationships with your audience. This, in turn, can lead to increased engagement, loyalty, and conversions for your brand or business.

## VI. Leveraging Audience Insights for Content Creation

### A. Tailoring Content Messaging and Tone

Tailoring content messaging and tone involves adapting your communication style to resonate with your audience's preferences, values, and communication styles. The messaging and tone of your content play a crucial role in capturing your audience's attention, building rapport, and fostering engagement. To effectively tailor content messaging and tone:

a) Audience Persona Alignment: Ensure that your messaging and tone align with the characteristics and preferences of your audience personas. Consider factors such as age, gender, language proficiency, and cultural background when crafting your content.

b) Brand Voice Consistency: Maintain consistency in your brand voice across all content channels while adjusting the messaging and tone to suit different audience segments. Your brand voice should reflect your brand personality and values while resonating with your audience's preferences.

c) Emotional Resonance: Incorporate emotional triggers and storytelling techniques that resonate with your audience's emotions and aspirations. Use language and imagery that evoke the desired emotional response and connect with your audience on a deeper level.

d) Empathy and Understanding: Demonstrate empathy and understanding towards your audience's needs, challenges, and aspirations in your content messaging. Show that you understand their pain points and are committed to providing solutions that meet their needs.

## B. Creating Content that Resonates with Audience Segments

Creating content that resonates with audience segments involves tailoring your content to address the specific interests, preferences, and needs of different audience segments. By understanding the unique characteristics and motivations of each audience segment, you can create content that speaks directly to their concerns and aspirations. To create content that resonates with audience segments:

a) Segment-Specific Content: Develop content that is tailored to the interests and preferences of each audience segment identified through audience research. Consider creating content clusters or content series targeting specific audience segments to provide a more personalised experience.

b) Relevant and Timely Topics: Identify trending topics, industry news, and events that are relevant to each audience segment and incorporate them into your content strategy. Stay updated on changes in audience preferences and adjust your content topics accordingly to maintain relevance.

c) Content Format Variety: Offer a variety of content formats and mediums that cater to different audience preferences and consumption habits. Experiment with video, audio, written content, infographics, and interactive content to appeal to diverse audience segments.

d) Personalisation and Customisation: Use personalisation techniques to customise content recommendations and experiences based on individual user preferences and behaviours. Tailor content recommendations, product suggestions, and messaging based on user interactions and engagement data.

## C. Incorporating Audience Feedback and Iterating Content Strategies

Incorporating audience feedback and iterating content strategies involves listening to your audience's feedback, analysing data, and making continuous improvements to your content based on insights gained. By actively seeking feedback and adapting your content strategies accordingly, you can ensure that your content remains relevant, engaging, and effective. To incorporate audience feedback and iterate content strategies:

a) Feedback Collection Mechanisms: Implement feedback collection mechanisms such as surveys, polls, comment sections, and customer feedback forms to gather insights from your audience. Encourage open communication and feedback sharing to foster a culture of continuous improvement.

b) Data Analysis and Insights: Analyse audience engagement metrics, content performance data, and audience feedback to identify trends, patterns, and areas for improvement. Use analytics tools and dashboards to track key performance indicators and monitor changes in audience behaviour.

c) Iterative Testing and Optimisation: Experiment with different content formats, messaging strategies, and distribution channels through A/B testing and iterative optimisation. Test variations of content elements such as headlines, images, calls-to-action, and delivery timing to determine what resonates best with your audience.

d) Collaboration and Cross-Functional Alignment: Foster collaboration and cross-functional alignment between content creators, marketers, data analysts, and customer support teams to leverage diverse perspectives and expertise. Share insights and learnings across teams to inform content strategies and drive continuous improvement.

By incorporating audience feedback and iterating content strategies based on insights gained, you can ensure that your content remains relevant, engaging, and impactful, ultimately driving better results for your brand or business.

## VII. Testing and Optimisation

### A. A/B Testing Content Variations

A/B testing content variations is a systematic approach to experiment with different elements of your content to determine which version performs better with your audience. By conducting A/B tests, you can identify the most effective content elements and optimise your content strategy to maximise engagement, conversions, and overall effectiveness.

To conduct A/B testing of content variations:

a) Define Test Objectives: Clearly define the objectives of your A/B test, whether it's to improve click-through rates, increase conversions, or enhance engagement metrics. Establish key performance indicators (KPIs) to measure the success of each content variation.

b) Identify Test Variables: Determine the specific elements of your content that you want to test, such as headlines, images, call-to-action buttons, or content layout. Create variations of these elements to test different hypotheses or strategies.

c) Split Test Audience: Divide your audience into two or more segments and randomly assign each segment to receive one of the content variations. Ensure that the test groups are comparable in size and composition to obtain reliable results.

d) Measure and Analyse Results: Track relevant performance metrics for each content variation, such as click-through rates, conversion rates, time on page, or bounce rates. Use statistical analysis to determine whether any differences in performance are statistically significant.

e) Draw Conclusions and Implement Changes: Analyse the results of the A/B test to identify the winning variation(s) that outperform the others. Implement the changes based on the insights gained from the A/B test and monitor the impact on performance metrics over time.

A/B testing content variations allows you to make data-driven decisions and continuously optimise your content strategy to better resonate with your audience and achieve your marketing objectives.

## B. Analysing Content Performance Metrics

Analysing content performance metrics is essential for evaluating the effectiveness of your content and identifying areas for improvement. By tracking key performance indicators (KPIs) and analysing content performance metrics, you can gain insights into how well your content resonates with your audience, drives engagement, and contributes to your overall marketing goals.

Key content performance metrics to analyse include:

a) Traffic Metrics: Track metrics such as page views, unique visitors, and sessions to measure the volume of traffic driven to your content.

b) Engagement Metrics: Measure engagement metrics such as bounce rate, time on page, scroll depth, and social shares to assess how effectively your content captures and maintains your audience's attention.

c) Conversion Metrics: Monitor conversion metrics such as conversion rate, click-through rate, and lead generation to evaluate how well your content drives desired actions and contributes to your conversion goals.

d) Audience Behaviour Metrics: Analyse audience behaviour metrics such as exit rate, navigation paths, and user journey to understand how users interact with your content and identify opportunities for optimisation.

e) Content Quality Metrics: Assess content quality metrics such as readability, relevance, and comprehensiveness to ensure that your content meets the needs and expectations of your audience.

By analysing content performance metrics, you can identify trends, patterns, and opportunities for improvement, allowing you to refine your content strategy and optimise future content efforts.

## C. Iterating Content Strategies Based on Insights

Iterating content strategies based on insights involves using data-driven insights to refine and optimise your content strategy over time. By continuously monitoring content performance, gathering audience feedback, and analysing data, you can identify opportunities for improvement and make iterative adjustments to your content strategy to better resonate with your audience and achieve your marketing objectives.

Key steps in iterating content strategies based on insights include:

a) Regular Performance Review: Conduct regular reviews of content performance metrics to identify trends, patterns, and areas for improvement. Monitor changes in audience behaviour, engagement levels, and conversion rates to inform content strategy adjustments.

b) Audience Feedback Analysis: Analyse audience feedback from surveys, comments, reviews, and social media interactions to understand audience preferences, pain points, and preferences. Use this feedback to identify content gaps and opportunities for improvement.

c) Competitor Analysis: Monitor competitor content strategies and performance to identify emerging trends, benchmark performance metrics, and gain inspiration for content ideas and strategies.

d) Experimentation and Testing: Experiment with new content formats, topics, and distribution channels through A/B testing, multivariate testing, or pilot programs. Test hypotheses and iterate content strategies based on data-driven insights and learnings from experimentation.

e) Continuous Optimisation: Continuously optimise your content strategy based on insights gained from data analysis, audience feedback, and experimentation. Make iterative adjustments to content messaging, formats, distribution channels, and targeting strategies to improve performance and achieve marketing objectives.

By iteratively refining and optimising your content strategy based on insights, you can adapt to changing audience preferences, trends, and market dynamics, ultimately driving better results and maximising the impact of your content efforts.

## VIII. Case Studies and Examples

A. Real-World Examples of Audience Understanding in Action

Audience understanding is a cornerstone of successful content marketing, and many brands have leveraged deep insights into their target audience to create impactful campaigns. Here are some real-world examples of audience understanding in action:

*Nike's "Just Do It" Campaign*

Nike has long been known for its ability to connect with its audience on an emotional level. Their "Just Do It" campaign, launched in 1988, resonated with athletes and everyday people alike by tapping into the universal human desire for achievement and self-improvement. By understanding their audience's aspirations and motivations, Nike created a powerful message that continues to inspire audiences worldwide.

*Dove's "Real Beauty" Campaign*

Dove's "Real Beauty" campaign challenged traditional beauty standards and celebrated diversity by featuring real women of all shapes, sizes, and ethnicities in their advertisements. By acknowledging and embracing the diversity of their audience, Dove struck a chord with consumers who were tired of unrealistic beauty ideals promoted by the media. The campaign not only resonated with Dove's target audience but also sparked important conversations about body positivity and self-acceptance.

*Red Bull's Content Marketing Strategy*

Red Bull has built a brand synonymous with extreme sports and adrenaline-fueled activities by understanding their audience's passion for adventure and excitement. Through their content marketing efforts, including the Red Bull Media House and events like the Red Bull Stratos space jump, Red Bull has cultivated a loyal following of thrill-seekers and action sports enthusiasts. By consistently delivering high-quality content that aligns with their audience's interests, Red Bull has become one of the most recognisable brands in the world.

These examples demonstrate how brands can achieve remarkable success by understanding their audience's values, aspirations, and interests, and creating content that resonates with them on a deep level.

B. Case Studies Highlighting Successful Audience-Centric Content Marketing Campaigns

Successful content marketing campaigns are often characterised by their ability to put the audience front and centre, delivering value and relevance to meet their needs and preferences. Here are some case studies highlighting audience-centric content marketing campaigns:

*Airbnb's "Live There" Campaign*

Airbnb's "Live There" campaign focused on showcasing the unique experiences and local culture that travellers can enjoy by staying in Airbnb accommodations. By highlighting the idea of "living like a local," Airbnb tapped into the desire for authentic and immersive travel experiences. The campaign featured user-generated content and personalised recommendations based on individual preferences, resonating with travellers seeking unique and memorable experiences.

*Coca-Cola's "Share a Coke" Campaign*

Coca-Cola's "Share a Coke" campaign personalised the brand experience by replacing the Coca-Cola logo on its bottles with popular names and phrases. By inviting consumers to "share a Coke" with friends and family, Coca-Cola created a sense of connection and community around its products. The campaign generated widespread social media engagement as consumers shared photos of their personalised Coke bottles, effectively turning customers into brand ambassadors.

*Oreo's "Dunk in the Dark" Tweet*

During the 2013 Super Bowl blackout, Oreo capitalised on the moment by tweeting a simple image of an Oreo cookie with the caption "You can still dunk in the dark." The tweet quickly went viral, demonstrating Oreo's agility and ability to connect with its audience in real-time. By tapping into a cultural moment and showcasing their brand personality, Oreo effectively engaged with consumers and earned widespread acclaim for their creativity and wit.

These case studies illustrate how brands can achieve remarkable results by putting their audience at the centre of their content marketing efforts, delivering value, relevance, and authenticity that resonates with their target audience.

## IX. Conclusion

### A. Recap of Key Insights and Takeaways

Throughout this chapter, we've explored various aspects of understanding your audience in content marketing. Here's a recap of the key insights and takeaways:

a) Audience Persona Development: Creating detailed audience personas based on demographic, psychographic, and behavioural data helps tailor content to meet specific audience needs and preferences.

b) Identifying Pain Points and Challenges: Understanding audience pain points and challenges enables content creators to address these issues directly, providing valuable solutions and building trust with the audience.

c) Assessing Content Preferences and Formats: Analysing audience content preferences and formats allows content creators to deliver content in the most engaging and effective manner, meeting audience expectations and driving better results.

d) Incorporating Audience Feedback: Integrating audience feedback into content strategies fosters continuous improvement, ensuring that content remains relevant, resonant, and impactful over time.

e) A/B Testing and Data Analysis: Conducting A/B tests, analysing content performance metrics, and iterating content strategies based on insights enable content creators to optimise content for maximum effectiveness and engagement.

By incorporating these insights into your content marketing strategy, you can create content that truly resonates with your audience, drives engagement, and achieves your marketing objectives.

B. Importance of Ongoing Audience Understanding in Content Marketing Strategy

Audience understanding is not a one-time exercise but an ongoing process that requires continuous monitoring, analysis, and adaptation. Here's why ongoing audience understanding is crucial in content marketing strategy:

a) Changing Audience Preferences: Audience preferences, behaviours, and expectations evolve over time due to changes in technology, culture, and market dynamics. Ongoing audience understanding allows content creators to stay attuned to these changes and adapt their content strategies accordingly.

b) Competitive Landscape: The competitive landscape is constantly evolving, with new competitors entering the market and existing competitors refining their strategies. By continuously understanding audience preferences and behaviours, content creators can stay ahead of the competition and differentiate their offerings effectively.

c) Content Performance Optimisation: Content performance metrics provide valuable insights into what resonates with the audience and what doesn't. By continuously analysing content performance data and iterating content strategies based on insights, content creators can optimise content for maximum effectiveness and engagement.

d) Building Audience Relationships: Audience understanding is essential for building strong relationships with your audience based on trust, relevance, and authenticity. By demonstrating a deep understanding of their needs, preferences, and challenges, content creators can foster a sense of connection and loyalty with their audience over time.

C. Next Steps for Applying Audience Insights to Content Marketing Efforts

Now that you have a deeper understanding of your audience and their preferences, here are some next steps for applying audience insights to your content marketing efforts:

a) Content Planning and Creation: Use audience insights to inform content planning and creation, ensuring that content topics, formats, and messaging align with audience preferences and interests.

b) Content Distribution and Promotion: Tailor content distribution and promotion strategies to reach your target audience effectively through the channels and platforms they frequent most.

c) Content Optimisation and Iteration: Continuously monitor content performance metrics and iterate content strategies based on insights to optimise content for maximum engagement and effectiveness.

d) Audience Engagement and Feedback: Engage with your audience regularly through social media, surveys, and feedback mechanisms to gather insights, address concerns, and foster a sense of community.

By applying audience insights to your content marketing efforts in these ways, you can create content that resonates with your audience, drives engagement, and achieves your marketing objectives effectively.

# Chapter 3: Crafting Compelling Content

## I. Introduction to Crafting Compelling Content

### A. Overview of the Chapter's Purpose

In this chapter, we delve into the art and science of crafting compelling content that captivates audiences and drives meaningful engagement. From understanding the psychology behind content consumption to mastering storytelling techniques and leveraging various content formats and delivery channels, this chapter aims to equip you with the knowledge and skills needed to create content that resonates with your audience on a deeper level.

The purpose of this chapter is to provide a comprehensive overview of the key elements involved in crafting compelling content for audience engagement. By exploring topics such as content psychology, storytelling techniques, content formats, writing compelling copy, visual content creation, personalisation strategies, content curation, user-generated content, and content measurement, you will gain valuable insights and practical strategies for creating content that not only captures attention but also inspires action and fosters lasting connections with your audience.

Whether you're a seasoned content creator looking to refine your skills or a newcomer to the world of content marketing seeking guidance on where to begin, this chapter serves as a roadmap for crafting compelling content that drives meaningful results in audience engagement.

### B. Importance of Compelling Content in Audience Engagement

Compelling content is the lifeblood of successful audience engagement in content marketing. It serves as the bridge that connects brands with their target audiences, capturing attention, building trust, and inspiring action. Here's why compelling content is essential for audience engagement:

a) Capturing Attention: In today's information-saturated digital landscape, capturing and holding audience attention is more challenging than ever. Compelling content grabs the audience's attention from the outset and keeps them engaged throughout the content journey.

b) Building Trust and Credibility: Compelling content demonstrates expertise, authenticity, and reliability, building trust and credibility with the audience. When audiences trust the content they consume, they are more likely to engage with it and take desired actions.

c) Inspiring Action: Compelling content moves audiences to act, whether it's sharing the content with others, signing up for a newsletter, making a purchase, or participating in a brand's campaign. By tapping into audience emotions and motivations, compelling content inspires action and drives desired outcomes.

d) Fostering Connection and Loyalty: Compelling content creates a sense of connection and resonance with the audience, fostering long-term relationships and brand loyalty. When audiences feel understood, valued, and entertained by the content they consume, they are more likely to become loyal advocates and ambassadors for the brand.

e) Driving Results: Ultimately, compelling content drives tangible results in audience engagement, including increased website traffic, higher conversion rates, greater brand awareness, and enhanced customer loyalty. By investing in crafting compelling content, brands can achieve their marketing objectives and stand out in a crowded digital landscape.

In summary, compelling content is indispensable for audience engagement in content marketing, serving as the catalyst that sparks meaningful interactions, fosters connections, and drives results. By prioritising the creation of compelling content, brands can effectively engage with their audiences and achieve their marketing goals in today's competitive digital environment.

## II. Understanding Content Psychology

### A. The Psychology of Content Consumption

Understanding the psychology behind content consumption is crucial for crafting content that resonates with audiences and drives engagement. Here are key insights into the psychology of content consumption:

   a) Attention Economy: In an age of information overload, attention is a scarce commodity. Content consumers are selective about where they invest their attention, favouring content that is relevant, valuable, and engaging.

   b) Cognitive Load Theory: Content consumers have limited cognitive resources, and their ability to process information is finite. Content that is easy to understand, concise, and visually appealing reduces cognitive load and enhances comprehension and retention.

   c) Visual Processing: The human brain processes visual information more quickly and effectively than text. Incorporating visual elements such as images, videos, and infographics into content can capture attention, evoke emotions, and enhance understanding.

   d) Storytelling and Narratives: Stories are a powerful tool for engaging audiences and fostering emotional connections. Narrative structures such as conflict, resolution, and character development captivate attention, stimulate empathy, and enhance message recall.

## B. Leveraging Emotional Triggers in Content Creation

Emotions play a central role in driving content consumption and engagement. By leveraging emotional triggers in content creation, marketers can evoke powerful responses and forge deeper connections with their audience:

a) Emotional Resonance: Content that taps into universal emotions such as joy, fear, anger, sadness, or surprise resonates with audiences on a visceral level, eliciting strong emotional responses and increasing engagement.

b) Empathy and Understanding: Content that demonstrates empathy and understanding towards audience needs, challenges, and aspirations fosters emotional connections and builds trust and rapport with the audience.

c) Aspirational Messaging: Content that inspires and motivates audiences to aspire to a better version of themselves triggers positive emotions such as hope, inspiration, and optimism, driving engagement and loyalty.

d) Personalisation and Relevance: Personalised content that speaks directly to individual needs, preferences, and experiences resonates with audiences on a personal level, eliciting emotional responses and increasing engagement.

## C. Cognitive Biases and Their Impact on Content Effectiveness

Cognitive biases are systematic patterns of deviation from rationality in judgment and decision-making. Understanding cognitive biases can help content creators design content that aligns with audience cognitive processes and preferences:

a) Confirmation Bias: Audiences tend to seek out information that confirms their existing beliefs and opinions. Content that reinforces existing attitudes and beliefs resonates with audiences and reinforces their worldview.

b) Anchoring Bias: Audiences tend to rely heavily on the first piece of information encountered (the "anchor") when making decisions. Content that presents compelling arguments or persuasive messages early in the content can influence audience perception and decision-making.

c) Social Proof: Audiences are influenced by the actions and opinions of others. Content that incorporates social proof, such as testimonials, reviews, or user-generated content, leverages the psychological principle of social validation to increase credibility and trust.

d) Loss Aversion: Audiences are more motivated by the fear of loss than the potential for gain. Content that emphasises potential losses or missed opportunities can spur action and drive engagement by tapping into audiences' aversion to loss.

e) By understanding the psychology of content consumption, leveraging emotional triggers, and addressing cognitive biases, content creators can craft content that resonates with audiences, drives engagement, and achieves marketing objectives effectively.

III. Storytelling Techniques for Engaging Audiences

A. The Power of Storytelling in Content Marketing

Storytelling is not just an ancient tradition; it's a potent tool in the modern marketer's arsenal. Here's why storytelling is paramount in content marketing:

   a) Emotional Connection: Stories have a unique ability to evoke emotions, forging a deep and lasting connection with audiences. By tapping into universal human experiences, storytelling transcends mere information, resonating with audiences on a visceral level.

   b) Brand Identity and Values: Through storytelling, brands can convey their identity, values, and mission in a compelling narrative format. Stories offer a window into the soul of a brand, humanising it and fostering trust and loyalty among audiences.

   c) Engagement and Attention: In an age of constant digital noise, storytelling cuts through the clutter, capturing and holding the audience's attention. By crafting narratives that unfold over time, brands can captivate audiences, drawing them into the story and fostering engagement.

   d) Message Retention: Stories are inherently memorable, making them an effective vehicle for delivering key messages and information. By embedding messages within a narrative framework, brands can increase message retention and ensure that their content leaves a lasting impression.

B. Elements of Effective Storytelling

Effective storytelling relies on several key elements to create a compelling and memorable narrative:

   a) Character Development: Compelling stories feature well-rounded characters with distinct personalities, motivations, and arcs. By bringing characters to life, storytelling creates empathy and connection with audiences, driving engagement and investment in the narrative.

b) Conflict and Resolution: Conflict lies at the heart of every great story, driving the plot forward and keeping audiences engaged. Whether it's internal struggles, interpersonal conflicts, or external challenges, conflict creates tension and stakes that propel the narrative forward.

c) Setting and Atmosphere: The setting of a story serves as its backdrop, immersing audiences in a vivid and immersive world. By painting a richly detailed setting with evocative language and imagery, storytelling transports audiences to new realms and enriches the narrative experience.

d) Plot Structure: Effective stories follow a coherent plot structure, guiding audiences through a series of events with a clear beginning, middle, and end. From the inciting incident that sets the story in motion to the climax that resolves the central conflict, a well-crafted plot structure ensures that the narrative unfolds in a satisfying and impactful way.

## C. Incorporating Narrative Arcs in Content Creation

Narrative arcs provide a framework for structuring content in a way that maximises engagement and impact:

a) Exposition: Introduce the audience to the characters, setting, and context of the story, setting the stage for the narrative to unfold.

b) Rising Action: Build tension and momentum as the story progresses, introducing obstacles and challenges that the characters must overcome.

c) Climax: Reach the narrative's peak moment of tension and drama, where the central conflict is confronted and resolved in a decisive and impactful way.

d) Falling Action: Begin to wind down the story, resolving any remaining plot threads and providing closure to the narrative. This phase allows audiences to reflect on the story's resolution and its broader themes and messages.

e) By incorporating storytelling principles and narrative arcs into content creation, brands can create compelling and impactful narratives that resonate deeply with their audience, driving engagement, and fostering lasting connections.

## IV. Content Formats and Delivery Channels

A. Exploring Different Content Formats (e.g., Articles, Videos, Infographics)

Content creators have a plethora of formats at their disposal, each offering unique opportunities to engage with audiences:

a) Articles and Blog Posts: Written content remains a cornerstone of content marketing, offering in-depth exploration of topics, industry insights, and thought leadership. Articles and blog posts provide valuable information in a format that is easily consumable and shareable.

b) Videos: Video content has surged in popularity, offering a dynamic and engaging way to convey information, entertain, and inspire. From product demos and tutorials to brand storytelling and behind-the-scenes footage, videos captivate audiences and drive higher engagement rates.

c) Infographics: Infographics combine text, visuals, and data to communicate complex information in a visually compelling and easily digestible format. Infographics are highly shareable and can help brands distil key insights and statistics into visually appealing content that resonates with audiences.

d) Podcasts: Podcasts have emerged as a popular content format, offering audiences a convenient way to consume information and entertainment on the go. Podcasts provide a platform for storytelling, interviews, and discussions, allowing brands to connect with audiences in a more intimate and conversational manner.

## B. Choosing the Right Delivery Channels for Your Audience

Selecting the appropriate delivery channels is essential for reaching and engaging with your target audience effectively:

a) Website and Blog: Your website serves as your digital home base, providing a centralised hub for your content and brand messaging. A blog allows you to regularly publish fresh content, attract organic traffic, and establish thought leadership in your industry.

b) Social Media Platforms: Social media platforms offer a vast and diverse audience, making them ideal for expanding your reach and driving engagement. Choose social media channels that align with your target audience demographics, interests, and preferences, and tailor your content accordingly.

c) Email Marketing: Email remains one of the most effective channels for nurturing leads, building relationships, and driving conversions. Develop targeted email campaigns that deliver relevant content to your audience based on their interests, behaviours, and lifecycle stage.

d) Content Syndication: Syndicating your content on third-party platforms and publications can help you reach new audiences and amplify your brand's visibility. Identify reputable publishers and platforms within your niche and explore opportunities for content collaboration and syndication.

## C. Multichannel Content Distribution Strategies

A multichannel content distribution strategy maximises your reach and impact by leveraging multiple channels to distribute your content:

a) Omni-channel Approach: Adopt an omni-channel approach that ensures a consistent brand experience across all touchpoints and channels. Seamlessly integrate your content across different platforms, devices, and channels to create a cohesive and unified brand presence.

b) Content Repurposing: Repurpose your content across different formats and channels to extend its lifespan and reach new audiences. For example, transform blog posts into videos, podcasts into blog articles, or infographics into social media posts.

c) Cross-promotion: Cross-promote your content across your various channels to increase visibility and engagement. Share snippets, teasers, or excerpts of your content on social media, email newsletters, and other platforms to drive traffic back to your website or blog.

d) Performance Monitoring and Optimisation: Continuously monitor the performance of your content across different channels and platforms. Identify which channels are driving the most engagement and conversions and allocate resources accordingly to optimise your content distribution strategy.

By exploring different content formats, choosing the right delivery channels, and implementing multichannel distribution strategies, brands can effectively reach and engage their target audience, drive traffic and conversions, and ultimately achieve their marketing objectives.

## V. Writing Compelling Copy and Headlines

### A. Crafting Attention-Grabbing Headlines

Headlines are the gateway to your content, enticing readers to click and engage. Here's how to craft headlines that capture attention:

a) Be Clear and Concise: Keep your headlines clear and concise, communicating the main idea or benefit of the content in a few words. Avoid ambiguity or jargon that may confuse readers.

b) Use Powerful Words: Incorporate strong, action-oriented words that evoke emotion and intrigue. Words like "discover," "uncover," "transform," or "ultimate" can grab attention and pique curiosity.

c) Create a Sense of Urgency: Include words or phrases that create a sense of urgency or scarcity, encouraging readers to act quickly. Terms like "limited time offer," "act now," or "don't miss out" can compel readers to click on your headline.

d) Invoke Curiosity: Pose a question or tease a surprising or intriguing fact to spark curiosity and compel readers to learn more. Curiosity-driven headlines prompt readers to click to satisfy their curiosity and uncover the answer.

### B. Writing Persuasive Copy that Drives Action

Effective copywriting goes beyond mere description; it persuades readers to take action. Here are key strategies for writing persuasive copy:

a) Know Your Audience: Tailor your copy to resonate with your target audience's needs, desires, and pain points. Speak directly to their aspirations, fears, and motivations to establish a connection and build trust.
b) Highlight Benefits, Not Features: Focus on the benefits that your product or service offers rather than listing its features. Clearly communicate how your offering solves a problem or fulfils a need for the reader, Emphasising the value it provides.

c) Use Social Proof: Incorporate social proof, such as customer testimonials, case studies, or endorsements, to build credibility and trust. Demonstrating that others have benefited from your product or service can persuade readers to take action.

d) Create a Compelling Call to Action (CTA): Clearly articulate the desired action you want readers to take, whether it's making a purchase, signing up for a newsletter, or downloading a resource. Use persuasive language and a sense of urgency to encourage immediate action.

## C. Tips for Optimising Copy for SEO and Readability

Optimising your copy for search engines and readability ensures that it reaches and resonates with your target audience:

a) Keyword Research: Conduct keyword research to identify relevant keywords and phrases that your audience is searching for. Incorporate these keywords naturally throughout your copy to improve its visibility in search engine results.

b) Write for Humans, Not Search Engines: While it's essential to include keywords for SEO, prioritise writing content that is valuable and engaging for your human audience. Focus on providing useful information and solving problems to keep readers engaged.

c) Break Up Text: Use short paragraphs, bullet points, and subheadings to break up large blocks of text and improve readability. Readers are more likely to skim content online, so make it easy for them to find and digest key information.

d) Optimise Meta Tags: Write compelling meta titles and descriptions that accurately describe the content and entice readers to click. Include relevant keywords in your meta tags to improve visibility in search engine results pages (SERPs).

By crafting attention-grabbing headlines, writing persuasive copy, and optimising copy for SEO and readability, brands can create content that not only captures attention but also drives action and achieves marketing objectives effectively.

## VI. Visual Content Creation Strategies

### A. Importance of Visual Content in Audience Engagement

Visual content has become increasingly crucial in capturing and maintaining audience attention. Here's why it's so vital:

a) Enhanced Engagement: Visuals, such as images, videos, and infographics, are more engaging and memorable than text alone. They attract attention and convey information quickly and effectively, making them ideal for capturing audience interest.

b) Increased Shareability: Visual content is highly shareable on social media platforms, leading to greater reach and visibility for brands. Eye-catching visuals are more likely to be shared, liked, and commented on, extending the reach of your content to a wider audience.

c) Improved Comprehension: Visuals aid in information retention and comprehension. Complex concepts can be simplified and conveyed more effectively through visuals, helping audiences grasp key messages and ideas more easily.

d) Brand Identity and Recognition: Consistent use of visual elements helps reinforce brand identity and recognition. Visuals convey brand personality, values, and messaging, fostering a stronger connection with the audience and enhancing brand recall.

## B. Design Principles for Creating Visually Compelling Content

To create visually compelling content, consider the following design principles:

a) Simplicity: Keep designs clean and uncluttered to avoid overwhelming the viewer. Use white space effectively to guide the viewer's eye and focus attention on key elements.

b) Consistency: Maintain consistency in visual elements such as colours, fonts, and imagery to reinforce brand identity and create a cohesive visual experience across all content.

c) Hierarchy: Establish a visual hierarchy to prioritise information and guide the viewer's attention. Use size, colour, and placement to emphasise important elements and create a clear flow of information.

d) Balance: Achieve visual balance by distributing elements evenly throughout the design. Balance can be symmetrical, where elements are mirrored on either side of a central axis, or asymmetrical, where elements are balanced through contrast and visual weight.

## C. Tools and Resources for Creating Visual Content

Numerous tools and resources are available to assist in the creation of visually compelling content:

a) Graphic Design Tools: Platforms like Adobe Photoshop, Illustrator, and Canva offer powerful tools for creating graphics, illustrations, and designs from scratch or using customisable templates.

b) Video Editing Software: Software such as Adobe Premiere Pro, Final Cut Pro, and iMovie enable users to edit and produce professional-quality videos, incorporating effects, transitions, and audio enhancements.

c) Infographic Builders: Tools like Piktochart, Venngage, and Infogram allow users to create visually appealing infographics by combining charts, graphs, and illustrations with text and imagery.

d) Stock Photo Libraries: Access royalty-free images and illustrations from stock photo libraries such as Shutterstock, Adobe Stock, and Unsplash to enhance your visual content with professional-quality imagery.

By leveraging the importance of visual content in audience engagement, applying design principles for creating visually compelling content, and Utilising tools and resources for visual content creation, brands can enhance their content marketing efforts and effectively connect with their audience in a visually driven digital landscape.

## VII. Personalised Content Strategies

### A. Understanding the Importance of Personalised Content

Personalised content is paramount in today's marketing landscape for several reasons:

a) Enhanced Relevance: Personalised content resonates more deeply with individual audience members by addressing their specific needs, interests, and preferences. This relevance increases engagement and fosters stronger connections with the brand.

b) Improved Customer Experience: Personalisation enhances the customer experience by delivering content that feels tailor-made for the individual. By providing relevant recommendations and information, brands can delight customers and increase satisfaction.

c) Increased Conversions: Personalised content drives higher conversion rates by delivering the right message to the right person at the right time. By aligning content with the recipient's stage in the buyer's journey and addressing their pain points, personalised content encourages action and drives results.

d) Brand Loyalty and Advocacy: By demonstrating an understanding of their audience's needs and preferences, brands can build trust and loyalty among customers. Personalised experiences foster a sense of connection and appreciation, leading to increased brand advocacy and word-of-mouth referrals.

## B. Strategies for Segmenting Audiences for Personalisation

Segmenting your audience allows you to tailor content to specific groups based on shared characteristics or behaviours. Here are strategies for effective audience segmentation:

a) Demographic Segmentation: Divide your audience based on demographic factors such as age, gender, location, income, or occupation. Demographic segmentation provides insights into the characteristics and preferences of different audience segments.

b) Behavioural Segmentation: Segment your audience based on their actions, behaviours, or interactions with your brand. Behavioural segmentation may include factors such as purchase history, website activity, email engagement, or social media interactions.

c) Psychographic Segmentation: Segment your audience based on psychological factors such as attitudes, values, interests, and lifestyle choices. Psychographic segmentation provides insights into the motivations and preferences driving consumer behaviour.

d) Lifecycle Stage Segmentation: Segment your audience based on where they are in the customer lifecycle, such as new leads, active customers, or lapsed customers. Tailor content to address the unique needs and challenges of each stage in the customer journey.

## C. Dynamic Content Creation Techniques

Dynamic content allows you to create personalised experiences at scale by automatically adapting content based on individual user data. Here are techniques for dynamic content creation:

a) Personalised Recommendations: Use algorithms to recommend products, services, or content based on individual user preferences, browsing history, or purchase behaviour.

b) Dynamic Email Content: Create email campaigns with dynamic content blocks that change based on recipient data, such as location, past purchases, or behavioural triggers.

c) Website Personalisation: Customise website content and messaging based on visitor data, such as geographic location, referral source, or browsing behaviour.

d) Behavioural Triggers: Set up automated triggers that deliver targeted content or messaging based on specific user actions or behaviours, such as abandoning a cart, completing a purchase, or signing up for a newsletter.

By understanding the importance of personalised content, implementing effective audience segmentation strategies, and employing dynamic content creation techniques, brands can deliver highly relevant and engaging experiences that resonate with their audience and drive business results.

## VIII. Content Repurposing and Curation

### A. Leveraging Existing Content for Audience Engagement

Repurposing existing content offers numerous benefits for audience engagement:

a) Maximising Reach: Repurposing content allows brands to extend the lifespan of their existing content assets, reaching new audiences and driving additional engagement over time.

b) Reinforcing Messaging: Repurposing content across different formats and channels reinforces key messaging and brand identity, ensuring consistency and coherence in communication efforts.

c) Optimising Resources: Repurposing content enables brands to make the most of their resources by leveraging existing assets to create new content quickly and cost-effectively.

d) Enhancing SEO: Repurposing content can improve search engine optimisation (SEO) by increasing the volume of indexed pages and generating backlinks from other sites.

### B. Best Practices for Content Curation

Content curation involves selecting and sharing third-party content that is relevant and valuable to your audience. Here are best practices for effective content curation:

a) Define Your Audience: Understand the interests, preferences, and needs of your target audience to curate content that resonates with them and adds value to their experience.

b) Curate Diverse Content: Curate a diverse range of content types, formats, and sources to provide a well-rounded and comprehensive view of your industry or niche.

c) Add Value: Provide context, commentary, or insights when sharing curated content to add value and demonstrate your expertise to your audience.

d) Credit Sources: Always give credit to the original source when sharing curated content, respecting intellectual property rights and building trust with your audience.

## C. Strategies for Repurposing Content Across Different Channels

Repurposing content across different channels allows brands to reach and engage audiences on their preferred platforms. Here are strategies for repurposing content effectively:

a) Identify Evergreen Content: Identify evergreen content that remains relevant and valuable to your audience over time. Repurpose evergreen content into different formats such as blog posts, videos, podcasts, or infographics to reach new audiences and reinforce messaging.

b) Tailor Content for Each Channel: Adapt content to suit the unique characteristics and requirements of each channel. Customise messaging, formatting, and visuals to align with the preferences and expectations of the audience on each platform.

c) Create Content Series: Develop content series or themes that explore a topic or theme in-depth across multiple channels. Repurpose content into serialised formats such as blog series, video playlists, or social media campaigns to sustain audience engagement over time.

d) Promote Across Channels: Cross-promote repurposed content across different channels to maximise visibility and engagement. Share links, excerpts, or teasers of repurposed content on social media, email newsletters, and other platforms to drive traffic and engagement.

By leveraging existing content for audience engagement, practicing effective content curation, and implementing strategies for repurposing content across different channels, brands can optimise their content marketing efforts, reach new audiences, and drive meaningful engagement and conversions.

## IX. User-Generated Content Strategies

### A. Harnessing the Power of User-Generated Content

User-generated content (UGC) can be a valuable asset for brands in several ways:

a) Authenticity: UGC provides authentic and genuine insights into the experiences, opinions, and perspectives of real customers, enhancing the credibility and trustworthiness of the brand.

b) Engagement: UGC encourages active participation and engagement from your audience, fostering a sense of community and belonging among users who contribute content.

c) Social Proof: UGC serves as powerful social proof, demonstrating to potential customers that others have had positive experiences with the brand's products or services, thereby influencing purchasing decisions.

d) Content Variety: UGC adds diversity and variety to your content strategy, offering a range of perspectives, formats, and styles that appeal to different segments of your audience.

### B. Encouraging User Participation and Engagement

Encouraging user participation and engagement is essential for generating UGC:

a) Create Opportunities: Provide clear opportunities and incentives for users to create and share content, such as contests, challenges, or interactive campaigns that encourage participation.

b) Facilitate Sharing: Make it easy for users to contribute content by providing clear instructions, user-friendly submission processes, and accessible platforms for sharing, such as social media channels or branded hashtags.

c) Showcase UGC: Highlight and showcase UGC prominently on your website, social media channels, or marketing materials to Recognise and celebrate contributors and encourage further participation from others.

d) Engage with Contributors: Acknowledge and engage with users who contribute UGC by responding to comments, thanking them for their contributions, and fostering a sense of community and appreciation.

## C. Moderation and Management of User-Generated Content

Effective moderation and management of UGC are essential to maintain brand integrity and compliance:

a) Establish Guidelines: Establish clear guidelines and rules for acceptable UGC, outlining expectations for content quality, relevance, and appropriateness. Communicate these guidelines to users to ensure compliance.

b) Monitor and Review: Regularly monitor and review UGC to ensure it aligns with brand values and guidelines. Implement moderation tools and processes to filter out inappropriate or off-brand content.

c) Respond Appropriately: Respond promptly and appropriately to any issues or concerns related to UGC, such as addressing negative feedback or resolving disputes. Transparency and responsiveness are key to maintaining trust and credibility.

d) Legal Considerations: Be aware of legal considerations related to UGC, such as copyright, privacy, and intellectual property rights. Obtain necessary permissions or rights for content usage and ensure compliance with relevant regulations and laws.

By harnessing the power of user-generated content, encouraging user participation and engagement, and effectively moderating and managing UGC, brands can leverage the authentic voices of their customers to enhance brand perception, foster community, and drive meaningful engagement and loyalty.

## X. Content Performance Measurement and Optimisation

### A. Key Metrics for Evaluating Content Performance

Evaluating content performance requires tracking key metrics to gauge effectiveness and impact:

a) Engagement Metrics: Measure engagement metrics such as likes, shares, comments, and time spent on page to assess how well your content resonates with your audience and encourages interaction.

b) Reach and Visibility: Track metrics related to reach and visibility, such as impressions, clicks, and website traffic, to understand the extent to which your content is reaching and attracting audiences.

c) Conversion Metrics: Evaluate conversion metrics such as click-through rates, conversion rates, and lead generation to assess how effectively your content drives desired actions and contributes to business objectives.

d) Audience Insights: Gather audience insights such as demographics, interests, and behaviour to better understand your audience and tailor content to their preferences and needs.

## B. Tools and Analytics Platforms for Content Measurement

Several tools and analytics platforms are available to help measure and analyse content performance:

- a) Google Analytics: Google Analytics provides a comprehensive suite of tools for tracking website traffic, user behaviour, and conversion metrics. Use features such as event tracking, goal tracking, and custom dashboards to measure content performance effectively.

- b) Social Media Analytics: Social media platforms offer built-in analytics tools for tracking engagement metrics, reach, and audience demographics. Platforms like Facebook Insights, Twitter Analytics, and LinkedIn Analytics provide valuable insights into content performance on social channels.

- c) Content Management Systems (CMS): Many CMS platforms offer built-in analytics and reporting features that allow you to track content performance directly within the platform. WordPress, for example, offers plugins and integrations for monitoring website traffic and user behaviour.

- d) Third-Party Analytics Tools: Explore third-party analytics tools and platforms designed specifically for content measurement and optimisation, such as BuzzSumo, SEMrush, or Sprout Social. These tools offer advanced analytics, competitive analysis, and insights into content trends and performance.

## C. Iterative Optimisation Based on Performance Insights

Optimising content performance requires continuous monitoring and iterative improvement based on performance insights:

- a) Data Analysis: Regularly analyse content performance data to identify trends, patterns, and areas for improvement. Look for opportunities to optimise content based on what resonates most with your audience.

b) A/B Testing: Experiment with different content formats, headlines, visuals, and calls to action using A/B testing or split testing. Measure the impact of changes on key metrics and iterate based on performance results.

c) Content Iteration: Use performance insights to inform content iteration and refinement. Update existing content based on audience feedback, changing trends, or new information to keep it relevant and impactful over time.

d) Continuous Learning: Stay informed about industry best practices, emerging trends, and new technologies in content marketing and measurement. Continuously refine your strategies and tactics based on evolving audience preferences and market dynamics.

By identifying key metrics for evaluating content performance, leveraging tools and analytics platforms for measurement, and iteratively optimising content based on performance insights, brands can maximise the impact of their content marketing efforts and drive meaningful results.

## XI. Conclusion: Applying Content Strategies

### A. Recap of Key Insights and Strategies

Throughout this chapter, we've explored various insights and strategies to enhance your content marketing efforts:

a) Understanding Your Audience: We discussed the importance of audience understanding and segmentation, as well as techniques for gathering audience data and creating audience personas.

b) Crafting Compelling Content: We delved into the psychology of content consumption, the power of storytelling, and strategies for creating visually engaging and persuasive content.

c) Personalised Content Strategies: We examined the significance of personalised content, effective audience segmentation, and dynamic content creation techniques.

d) Content Repurposing and Curation: We explored the benefits of repurposing existing content, best practices for content curation, and strategies for repurposing content across different channels.

e) User-Generated Content Strategies: We highlighted the value of user-generated content, methods for encouraging user participation, and best practices for moderation and management.

f) Content Performance Measurement and Optimisation: We discussed key metrics for evaluating content performance, tools and analytics platforms for measurement, and iterative optimisation based on performance insights.

## B. Encouragement for Applying Techniques in Content Creation

Now that you've gained insights into these content marketing strategies, I encourage you to apply them in your content creation efforts. Whether you're crafting blog posts, videos, social media content, or email campaigns, consider how you can incorporate personalised elements, leverage user-generated content, and optimise for performance to maximise the impact of your content.

Experiment with different formats, styles, and messaging techniques to engage your audience and drive desired actions. Don't be afraid to iterate and refine your approach based on performance data and audience feedback.

Remember that effective content creation is an ongoing process of experimentation, learning, and adaptation. By embracing creativity and innovation, you can continually improve the quality and effectiveness of your content to achieve your marketing goals.

C. Looking Ahead to Implementing Content Strategies in the Next Chapters

As we move forward into the next chapters, we'll build upon the foundation established in this section to delve deeper into specific content marketing strategies and tactics. We'll explore topics such as content distribution, social media marketing, email marketing, SEO strategies, and more.

I encourage you to continue your journey with an open mind and a willingness to explore new ideas and techniques. By implementing the content strategies discussed in this chapter and remaining adaptable and responsive to changing trends and audience preferences, you'll be well-positioned to succeed in today's dynamic digital landscape.

## Chapter 4: Leveraging Distribution Channels

### I. Introduction to Distribution Channels

#### A. Definition and Importance

Distribution channels refer to the various avenues through which content is disseminated to target audiences. They play a crucial role in content marketing by facilitating the delivery of content to the right people at the right time.

Importance:

a) Reach and Visibility: Distribution channels amplify the reach and visibility of content, ensuring it reaches a broader audience.

b) Audience Engagement: They provide platforms for engaging with audiences, fostering interaction and conversation around content.

c) Conversion Opportunities: Distribution channels offer opportunities for converting audience engagement into desired actions, such as website visits, lead generation, or sales.

d) Brand Building: They contribute to brand building by reinforcing messaging, values, and identity across different touchpoints.

#### B. Overview of Distribution Channel Types

Distribution channels can be categorised into three main types:

**1. Owned Channels:**

a) Website and Blog: Owned digital properties where brands have full control over content creation and distribution.

b) Email Marketing: Direct communication channel with subscribers, delivering personalised content and updates.

c) Social Media Profiles: Brand-owned social media accounts used to share content and engage with followers.

**2. Earned Channels:**

a) Social Media Mentions and Shares: Organic mentions and shares of content by users on social media platforms.

b) Influencer Partnerships: Collaboration with influencers to amplify content reach and credibility.

c) Press Coverage: Media coverage and mentions of brand content or initiatives by third-party publications.

**3. Paid Channels:**

a) Paid Social Media Advertising: Targeted advertising on social media platforms to reach specific audience segments.

b) Search Engine Marketing (SEM): Paid search advertising to appear prominently in search engine results for relevant keywords.

c) Display Advertising: Banner ads and visual ads displayed on websites and online platforms to promote content or products.

Understanding the characteristics and capabilities of each distribution channel type is essential for developing an effective content distribution strategy that maximises reach, engagement, and conversion opportunities.

## II. Understanding Distribution Channel Options

A. Owned Channels

Owned channels are digital properties directly controlled by the brand, providing platforms for content creation, distribution, and engagement.

*Website and Blog*

Websites and blogs serve as central hubs for brands to showcase their products, services, and expertise. They offer a versatile platform for publishing various types of content, including articles, videos, infographics, and more. Websites and blogs play a crucial role in driving organic traffic, establishing authority, and nurturing relationships with visitors through valuable and informative content.

*Email Marketing*

Email marketing remains one of the most effective channels for nurturing leads and engaging existing customers. Brands use email campaigns to deliver personalised content, updates, promotions, and exclusive offers directly to subscribers' inboxes. Email marketing allows for segmentation and targeting based on subscriber preferences and behaviours, making it a powerful tool for driving conversions and building customer loyalty.

*Social Media Profiles*

Social media profiles provide brands with platforms to connect and engage with their audience on popular social networking sites such as Facebook, Instagram, Twitter, LinkedIn, and more. Social media profiles enable brands to share content, interact with followers, respond to comments and messages, and build communities around their brand. Leveraging social media profiles effectively can enhance brand visibility, foster engagement, and drive traffic to other owned channels such as websites and blogs.

## B. Earned Channels

Earned channels involve the organic promotion of content through mentions, shares, and endorsements by third-party sources.

*Social Media Mentions and Shares*

Social media mentions and shares occur when users interact with brand content on social media platforms by tagging, mentioning, or sharing it with their followers. These organic interactions increase content visibility, credibility, and reach, as they are perceived as genuine endorsements from real users.

*Influencer Partnerships*

Influencer partnerships involve collaborating with individuals or personalities who have significant influence and reach within a specific niche or industry. By partnering with influencers, brands can leverage their credibility, expertise, and audience engagement to amplify content reach, drive traffic, and build brand awareness.

*Press Coverage*

Press coverage refers to media mentions, reviews, or features of brand content or initiatives by third-party publications, journalists, or media outlets. Positive press coverage enhances brand credibility, authority, and visibility, as it provides independent validation and endorsement of brand content or offerings.

## C. Paid Channels

Paid channels involve the use of advertising and promotional tactics to reach and engage target audiences.

*Paid Social Media Advertising*

Paid social media advertising entails the use of paid promotions and sponsored content on social media platforms to target specific audience segments based on demographics, interests, and behaviours. Paid social media ads enable brands to increase content visibility, drive website traffic, generate leads, and boost conversions.

*Search Engine Marketing (SEM)*

Search engine marketing (SEM) involves the use of paid search advertising to appear prominently in search engine results pages (SERPs) for relevant keywords and queries. SEM allows brands to target users actively searching for specific products, services, or information, driving highly qualified traffic to their websites and landing pages.

*Display Advertising*

Display advertising encompasses various visual ad formats displayed on websites, mobile apps, and online platforms to promote brand content, products, or services. Display ads can include banner ads, rich media ads, video ads, and interactive ads, strategically placed to capture audience attention and drive engagement.

Understanding the characteristics and capabilities of each distribution channel type is essential for developing a comprehensive content distribution strategy that maximises reach, engagement, and conversion opportunities across owned, earned, and paid channels.

## III. Tailoring Content for Different Distribution Channels

### A. Content Formats and Messaging

*Visual Content for Social Media*

Visual content is highly engaging and effective for capturing audience attention on social media platforms. Here are some key visual content formats and messaging strategies for social media:

a) Infographics: Condense complex information into visually appealing graphics that are easy to consume and share. Use infographics to educate your audience, present statistics, or explain processes in a visually engaging format.

b) Images and Graphics: Incorporate high-quality images, graphics, and illustrations to complement your social media posts and convey your brand's personality and message. Choose visuals that resonate with your audience and align with your brand aesthetic.

c) Videos: Leverage the power of video content to tell stories, demonstrate products, or engage your audience in a more dynamic and immersive way. Create short-form videos, live streams, or tutorials to spark interest and encourage interaction.

*Long-Form Content for Blogs and Newsletters*

Long-form content provides an opportunity to dive deeper into topics, provide in-depth analysis, and offer valuable insights to your audience. Here's how to optimise long-form content for blogs and newsletters:

a) Comprehensive Guides and How-to Articles: Create comprehensive guides, tutorials, and how-to articles that address common questions, challenges, or pain points faced by your audience. Offer practical advice, actionable tips, and step-by-step instructions to add value and establish authority.

b) In-depth Analysis and Thought Leadership: Share thought-provoking insights, industry trends, and expert opinions through long-form articles and opinion pieces. Position your brand as a thought leader in your niche by offering unique perspectives and original research.

c) Case Studies and Success Stories: Showcase real-life examples and success stories to illustrate the impact of your products or services. Share customer testimonials, case studies, and client success stories that demonstrate tangible results and build trust with your audience.

*Interactive Content for Email Marketing*

Interactive content encourages active engagement and participation from email subscribers, driving higher click-through rates and conversions. Here are some interactive content formats and messaging strategies for email marketing:

a) Quizzes and Surveys: Create interactive quizzes, polls, or surveys to gather feedback, insights, and preferences from your email subscribers. Use interactive elements to personalise content and tailor recommendations based on user responses.

b) Interactive Galleries and Carousels: Showcase product collections, featured content, or customer testimonials through interactive image galleries or carousels. Allow subscribers to explore and interact with multiple images or products directly within the email.

c) Interactive CTAs and Forms: Enhance email engagement with interactive calls-to-action (CTAs) and forms that prompt subscribers to take specific actions, such as signing up for a webinar, downloading a resource, or making a purchase. Use compelling visuals and persuasive messaging to encourage conversions.

B. Optimisation Techniques

*SEO Strategies for Website Content*

Search engine optimisation (SEO) is essential for improving the visibility and ranking of website content in search engine results pages (SERPs). Here are some optimisation techniques for website content:

a) Keyword Research: Identify relevant keywords and phrases that align with your content topics and target audience's search intent. Use keyword research tools to discover high-volume keywords, long-tail keywords, and related terms to incorporate into your content.

b) On-Page Optimisation: Optimise on-page elements such as titles, meta descriptions, headings, and URLs with target keywords to improve search engine visibility and click-through rates. Ensure content is well-structured, easy to read, and mobile-friendly for optimal user experience.

c) Quality Content Creation: Create high-quality, valuable content that addresses user queries, provides comprehensive information, and fulfils search intent. Publish regularly updated, evergreen content that remains relevant and valuable to your audience over time.

*A/B Testing for Paid Advertising*

A/B testing, also known as split testing, is a method of comparing two versions of a webpage or ad to determine which one performs better. Here's how to implement A/B testing for paid advertising campaigns:

a) Ad Copy Testing: Test different ad copy variations to identify which messaging resonates most with your target audience. Experiment with different headlines, calls-to-action, and value propositions to optimise ad performance.

b) Visual Element Testing: Evaluate the impact of visual elements such as images, videos, or graphics on ad engagement and conversion rates. Test different visuals to determine which ones attract attention and drive action.

c) Audience Segmentation Testing: Segment your audience based on demographics, interests, or behaviours, and test different ad creatives and messaging for each segment. Tailor ads to specific audience segments to increase relevance and effectiveness.

*Personalisation for Email Campaigns*

Personalisation enhances the relevance and effectiveness of email marketing campaigns by delivering tailored content and offers to individual subscribers. Here are some personalisation techniques for email campaigns:

a) Dynamic Content: Use dynamic content blocks to customise email content based on subscriber data such as demographics, purchase history, or browsing behaviour. Deliver personalised product recommendations, relevant content, or special offers based on user preferences.

b) Segmentation and Targeting: Segment your email list into smaller groups based on characteristics such as location, interests, or engagement level, and tailor content to each segment's preferences and needs. Send targeted emails that address specific audience segments with relevant messaging.

c) Triggered Emails: Set up triggered email campaigns that automatically send personalised messages in response to specific user actions or behaviours, such as welcome emails, abandoned cart reminders, or birthday offers. Use automation to deliver timely and relevant communications to subscribers throughout their customer journey.

By optimising content formats and messaging for different distribution channels and implementing optimisation techniques such as SEO strategies, A/B testing, and personalisation, brands can maximise the effectiveness of their content marketing efforts and drive meaningful engagement and conversions.

## IV. Developing a Distribution Channel Strategy

### A. Audience Analysis and Channel Selection

Before developing a distribution channel strategy, it's crucial to conduct audience analysis to understand your target audience's preferences, behaviours, and content consumption habits. Here's how to approach audience analysis and channel selection:

a) Define Your Target Audience: Clearly define your target audience based on demographics, psychographics, interests, and behaviours. Identify their needs, pain points, and preferences to tailor content and distribution channels accordingly.

b) Audience Research: Conduct in-depth audience research using various sources such as website analytics, social media insights, customer surveys, and market research reports. Gather data on audience demographics, online behaviour, content preferences, and platform usage patterns.

c) Channel Compatibility: Evaluate the compatibility of different distribution channels with your target audience's preferences and behaviours. Consider factors such as platform popularity, audience demographics, content format preferences, and engagement levels.

d) Channel Selection: Select distribution channels that align with your target audience's characteristics and content consumption habits. Choose channels where your audience is most active and engaged, whether it's social media platforms, email newsletters, blogs, or niche industry forums.

B. Content Calendar and Publishing Schedule

Once you've identified your target audience and selected appropriate distribution channels, it's essential to develop a content calendar and publishing schedule to ensure consistent and timely content delivery. Here's how to create a content calendar:

a) Content Planning: Plan content topics, themes, and formats based on audience interests, industry trends, and marketing objectives.

Align content with your distribution channel strategy and the specific requirements of each channel.

b) Content Calendar: Create a content calendar outlining the publishing schedule for each distribution channel. Use tools such as spreadsheets, project management software, or content management systems (CMS) to organise and manage content scheduling.

c) Frequency and Timing: Determine the frequency and timing of content publication for each channel based on audience preferences, engagement patterns, and platform algorithms. Consider factors such as peak times for audience activity, content freshness, and campaign timelines.

d) Content Repurposing: Explore opportunities for content repurposing and cross-channel promotion to maximise content reach and engagement. Repurpose existing content into different formats or adapt it for specific distribution channels to extend its lifespan and appeal to different audience segments.

## C. Integration and Cross-Promotion Strategies

Integration and cross-promotion involve leveraging multiple distribution channels to amplify content reach and engagement. Here are some integration and cross-promotion strategies to consider:

a) Cross-Channel Promotion: Promote content across multiple channels to reach a wider audience and increase visibility. Share blog posts on social media, include social media links in email newsletters, and cross-promote content between different owned channels.

b) Content Syndication: Syndicate content on third-party platforms, industry websites, or content aggregators to expand your reach and attract new audiences. Seek opportunities for guest blogging, content partnerships, or collaborations with influencers to reach new audiences and gain exposure.

c) Integrated Campaigns: Develop integrated marketing campaigns that span multiple channels and touchpoints to create a cohesive brand experience. Coordinate messaging, visuals, and calls-to-action across channels to reinforce brand identity and campaign objectives.

d) Data Sharing and Insights: Share audience insights and performance data between different distribution channels to inform content strategy and optimisation efforts. Use data analytics and tracking tools to measure cross-channel performance and identify opportunities for improvement.

By conducting audience analysis and selecting appropriate distribution channels, developing a content calendar and publishing schedule, and implementing integration and cross-promotion strategies, brands can create a cohesive distribution channel strategy that maximises content reach, engagement, and impact across various platforms and touchpoints.

## V. Measuring and Analysing Distribution Channel Performance

### A. Key Performance Indicators (KPIs)

To evaluate the effectiveness of distribution channels, it's essential to track key performance indicators (KPIs) that measure various aspects of content performance. Here are three categories of KPIs to consider:

*Engagement Metrics*

Engagement metrics measure how actively audiences interact with your content. Key engagement metrics include:

a) Likes, Shares, and Comments: Quantify the level of audience interaction and engagement with your content on social media platforms.

b) Click-Through Rate (CTR): Measure the percentage of users who click on a link or call-to-action within your content, indicating interest and engagement.

c) Time Spent on Page: Assess the average duration users spend consuming your content, indicating interest and engagement levels.

*Reach and Visibility Metrics*

Reach and visibility metrics quantify the extent to which your content is exposed to and viewed by your target audience. Key reach and visibility metrics include:

a) Impressions: Count the number of times your content is displayed to users, providing insight into overall exposure and potential reach.

b) Website Traffic: Track the volume of visitors to your website or landing pages from various distribution channels, indicating the effectiveness of content promotion and distribution.

c) Follower Growth: Monitor the growth of your audience or follower base on social media platforms, indicating increased brand visibility and audience reach.

*Conversion Metrics*

Conversion metrics measure the effectiveness of content in driving desired actions and outcomes. Key conversion metrics include:

a) Conversion Rate: Calculate the percentage of users who take a desired action, such as making a purchase, filling out a form, or subscribing to a newsletter, in response to your content.

b) Lead Generation: Measure the number of leads generated from content interactions, indicating the effectiveness of content in capturing audience interest and generating potential sales opportunities.

c) Revenue or Return on Investment (ROI): Evaluate the financial impact of content marketing efforts by tracking revenue generated or ROI attributed to specific content campaigns or distribution channels.

## B. Analytics Tools and Platforms

To track and analyse distribution channel performance, utilise a variety of analytics tools and platforms that provide valuable insights into audience behaviour and content effectiveness. Here are three essential analytics tools:

*Google Analytics*

Google Analytics is a powerful web analytics platform that provides comprehensive insights into website traffic, user behaviour, and content performance. Key features include:

a) Audience Demographics: Understand the characteristics and interests of your website visitors, helping tailor content and messaging to their preferences.

b) Traffic Sources: Identify which distribution channels drive the most traffic to your website, enabling optimisation of content promotion strategies.

c) Goal Tracking: Set up and track specific goals such as conversions, sign-ups, or downloads to measure the effectiveness of content in driving desired actions.

*Social Media Analytics*

Social media platforms offer built-in analytics tools that provide insights into audience engagement, reach, and performance of content. Key features include:

a) Engagement Metrics: Monitor likes, shares, comments, and other interactions to gauge audience engagement with your content.

b) Audience Insights: Understand the demographics, interests, and behaviours of your social media followers, informing content strategy and targeting.

c) Post Performance: Analyse the performance of individual posts or content campaigns to identify top-performing content and optimise future efforts.

*Email Marketing Platforms*

Email marketing platforms such as Mailchimp, Constant Contact, or HubSpot offer analytics features that track the performance of email campaigns and subscriber engagement. Key features include:

a) Open Rate and Click-Through Rate: Measure the percentage of email recipients who open your emails and click on links within them, indicating engagement and interest.

b) Subscriber Growth: Track changes in your email subscriber list size over time, identifying trends and opportunities for list expansion.

c) Conversion Tracking: Monitor conversions generated from email campaigns, such as purchases or form submissions, to assess campaign effectiveness and ROI.

By tracking key performance indicators (KPIs) related to engagement, reach, visibility, and conversions, and Utilising analytics tools such as Google Analytics, social media analytics, and email marketing platforms, brands can gain valuable insights into distribution channel performance and optimise content marketing efforts for maximum impact and effectiveness.

## VI. Optimisation and Iteration

### A. Continuous Monitoring and Analysis

Continuous monitoring and analysis are essential for evaluating the effectiveness of distribution channel strategies and content performance. Here's how to approach continuous monitoring and analysis:

a) Real-Time Monitoring: Utilise analytics tools and dashboards to monitor distribution channel performance in real-time. Keep track of key metrics such as engagement, reach, and conversions to identify trends and patterns as they occur.

b) Regular Reporting: Generate regular reports summarising distribution channel performance and content metrics. Review performance data periodically to assess progress towards goals and identify areas for improvement.

c) Identify Successes and Challenges: Analyse performance data to identify successful content campaigns and distribution strategies, as well as any challenges or areas for optimisation. Use insights gained from analysis to inform future content and distribution decisions.

### B. Iterative Testing and Refinement

Iterative testing and refinement involve experimenting with different content formats, messaging strategies, and distribution tactics to optimise performance over time. Here's how to approach iterative testing and refinement:

a) A/B Testing: Conduct A/B tests to compare different variations of content or distribution strategies and identify which performs better with your audience. Test variables such as headlines, visuals, calls-to-action, and distribution channels to refine your approach.

b) Content Experimentation: Experiment with different content formats, topics, and messaging approaches to determine what resonates most with your audience. Track performance metrics for each experiment and iterate based on insights gained.

c) Feedback and Iteration: Solicit feedback from your audience through surveys, comments, and social media interactions. Use feedback to refine content and distribution strategies, addressing audience preferences and needs.

## C. Adaptation to Changing Trends and Audience Preferences

To stay relevant and effective, it's essential to adapt to changing trends and audience preferences in content consumption and distribution. Here's how to adapt to changing trends and audience preferences:

a) Stay Informed: Keep abreast of industry trends, emerging technologies, and changes in audience behaviour. Monitor competitor activity and industry news to identify shifts in content consumption habits and distribution trends.

b) Flexibility and Agility: Maintain flexibility in your content and distribution strategies to adapt quickly to changing market conditions and audience preferences. Be prepared to pivot or adjust strategies based on new insights and developments.

c) Experimentation and Innovation: Embrace experimentation and innovation in content creation and distribution to stay ahead of the curve. Test new formats, platforms, and distribution tactics to explore untapped opportunities and reach new audiences.

By continuously monitoring and analysing distribution channel performance, conducting iterative testing and refinement, and adapting to changing trends and audience preferences, brands can optimise their content marketing efforts for maximum impact and effectiveness in engaging and resonating with their target audience.

## VII. Success in Distribution Channel Strategies

### A. Successful Distribution Channel Strategies

Successful distribution channel strategies are characterised by a combination of thoughtful planning, strategic execution, and continuous optimisation. Here are key components of successful distribution channel strategies:

a) Audience-Centric Approach: Prioritise the needs, preferences, and behaviours of your target audience when selecting distribution channels and creating content. Tailor your distribution strategy to align with audience interests and consumption habits.

b) Multi-Channel Presence: Diversify your distribution channels to reach audiences across multiple touchpoints and platforms. Maintain a presence on various channels, including owned, earned, and paid channels, to maximise visibility and engagement.

c) Consistent Brand Messaging: Maintain consistency in brand messaging and tone across all distribution channels to reinforce brand identity and messaging. Ensure that content resonates with your audience and aligns with your brand values and objectives.

d) Data-Driven Decision Making: Use data analytics and performance metrics to inform distribution channel strategy and content optimisation efforts. Continuously monitor performance, analyse data, and iterate based on insights to improve effectiveness.

e) Integration and Cross-Promotion: Integrate distribution channels and leverage cross-promotion opportunities to amplify content reach and engagement. Coordinate messaging, visuals, and calls-to-action across channels to create a cohesive brand experience.

## B. Lessons Learned and Best Practices

Reflecting on past experiences and lessons learned can provide valuable insights and inform future distribution channel strategies. Here are some lessons learned and best practices to consider:

a) Test and Learn Approach: Embrace a test and learn approach to distribution channel strategies, experimenting with different tactics, formats, and messaging to identify what resonates best with your audience.

b) Iterative Optimisation: Recognise that distribution channel strategies are not static and require ongoing optimisation. Continuously monitor performance metrics, analyse data, and refine strategies based on insights and feedback.

c) Adaptability and Agility: Stay adaptable and agile in response to changing market dynamics, audience preferences, and industry trends. Be willing to pivot or adjust distribution strategies as needed to remain relevant and effective.

d) Collaboration and Communication: Foster collaboration and communication between cross-functional teams involved in content creation, distribution, and analytics. Ensure alignment on objectives, priorities, and performance goals to optimise coordination and effectiveness.

e) Customer-Centric Mindset: Maintain a customer-centric mindset throughout the distribution channel strategy development process. Prioritise delivering value and meeting customer needs at every touchpoint to drive engagement and loyalty.

By implementing successful distribution channel strategies and incorporating lessons learned and best practices, brands can enhance their content marketing efforts, maximise reach and engagement, and ultimately achieve their business objectives.

## VIII. Conclusion: Maximising Distribution Channel Strategies

### A. Recap of Distribution Channel Strategies

In this chapter, we've explored the intricacies of distribution channel strategies in content marketing. We delved into the importance of understanding your audience, selecting the right channels, crafting compelling content, and leveraging analytics for optimisation. Here's a recap of the key strategies discussed:

a) Audience-Centric Approach: Prioritise your audience's preferences and behaviours when selecting distribution channels and creating content to ensure maximum engagement and resonance.

b) Multi-Channel Presence: Diversify your distribution channels to reach audiences across various platforms, including owned, earned, and paid channels, to maximise visibility and engagement.

c) Consistent Brand Messaging: Maintain consistency in brand messaging and tone across all distribution channels to reinforce brand identity and messaging and ensure alignment with audience expectations.

d) Data-Driven Decision Making: Utilise data analytics and performance metrics to inform distribution channel strategy and content optimisation efforts, continuously monitoring performance and iterating based on insights.

### B. Encouragement for Implementation and Experimentation

Now that we've discussed various distribution channel strategies, it's time to put them into action. Don't hesitate to experiment with different tactics, formats, and messaging to identify what resonates best with your audience. Remember, implementation is key to learning and improvement.

Embrace a culture of experimentation and innovation within your organisation. Encourage your team to explore new ideas, test hypotheses, and iterate based on results. By fostering a mindset of continuous improvement and learning, you can stay ahead of the curve and adapt to changing market dynamics.

### C. Looking Ahead to Further Refinement and Growth

As you embark on your content marketing journey, keep an eye on the horizon for opportunities for further refinement and growth. Distribution channel strategies are not static; they require ongoing optimisation and adaptation to remain effective in a rapidly evolving landscape.

Stay informed about industry trends, emerging technologies, and shifts in audience preferences to inform your distribution channel strategies. Be proactive in identifying areas for improvement and exploring new avenues for growth.

By staying agile, adaptable, and forward-thinking, you can continue to refine your distribution channel strategies, drive meaningful engagement, and achieve your business objectives in the ever-changing world of content marketing.

# Chapter 5: Fostering Community Engagement

I. Introduction to Community Engagement

A. Definition and Importance of Community Engagement

Community engagement refers to the process of building and nurturing relationships with a group of individuals who share common interests, goals, or experiences. In the context of content marketing, community engagement involves creating opportunities for meaningful interaction, collaboration, and participation among members of your target audience.

The importance of community engagement lies in its ability to foster a sense of belonging, loyalty, and trust among your audience. By cultivating a vibrant community around your brand, you can create a supportive environment where members feel valued, heard, and empowered. This not only enhances brand loyalty but also drives advocacy, word-of-mouth marketing, and long-term customer relationships.

Community engagement goes beyond transactional interactions; it's about building lasting connections and relationships with your audience. It allows you to tap into the collective wisdom, creativity, and insights of your community members, enabling you to better understand their needs, preferences, and pain points. Ultimately, community engagement can be a powerful driver of brand growth, innovation, and success.

B. Benefits of Building a Community Around Your Brand

a) Brand Loyalty and Advocacy: A strong community fosters loyalty and advocacy among its members, leading to increased brand affinity and positive word-of-mouth referrals.

b) Enhanced Customer Support: Communities provide a platform for members to seek help, share advice, and troubleshoot issues, improving overall customer support and satisfaction.

c) Market Insights and Feedback: Engaged communities offer valuable insights into customer preferences, behaviours, and trends, helping inform product development, marketing strategies, and business decisions.

d) Increased Engagement and Interaction: Community engagement drives active participation and interaction among members, leading to higher levels of engagement with your brand and content.

e) Brand Differentiation and Competitive Advantage: A vibrant community sets your brand apart from competitors by creating a unique value proposition based on shared values, interests, and experiences.

C. Overview of Chapter Objectives and Structure

In this chapter, we'll explore the fundamentals of community engagement in content marketing. We'll delve into the strategies, tactics, and best practices for building and nurturing a thriving community around your brand. Here's an overview of what to expect:

a) Understanding Your Community: We'll start by discussing how to identify and define your target community, analyse their needs and behaviours, and segment them for personalised engagement.

b) Building and Nurturing Community Relationships: Next, we'll explore strategies for establishing trust, creating valuable content, and encouraging participation and interaction within your community.

c) Leveraging Community Platforms and Tools: We'll then delve into choosing the right community platforms, implementing effective community management practices, and Utilising engagement tools and analytics.

d) Measuring and Analysing Community Engagement: We'll discuss key metrics for evaluating community engagement, analytics tools for tracking performance, and strategies for continuous monitoring and adaptation.

e) Cultivating a Culture of Engagement: Finally, we'll explore tactics for encouraging user-generated content, facilitating meaningful discussions, and empowering community advocates and brand ambassadors.

Through this exploration, you'll gain a deeper understanding of the importance of community engagement, the benefits of building a community around your brand, and the strategies for harnessing the power of community in content marketing.

## II. Understanding Your Community

### A. Identifying and Defining Your Target Community

Before you can engage with your community effectively, you need to clearly identify and define who your target community members are. Here's how to do it:

a) Define Your Audience: Start by defining the demographics, interests, and behaviours of your ideal community members. Who are they? What are their interests? Where do they spend their time online?

b) Identify Common Characteristics: Look for common characteristics among your existing audience members or potential customers. Are there shared demographics, such as age, gender, location, or occupation? Are there common interests or hobbies that unite them?

c) Research Audience Needs and Pain Points: Conduct research to understand the needs, challenges, and pain points of your target audience. What problems are they trying to solve? What questions do they have? What are their goals and aspirations?

## B. Analysing Community Needs, Interests, and Behaviours

Once you've identified your target community, it's essential to analyse their needs, interests, and behaviours to tailor your engagement efforts effectively. Here's how:

a) Conduct Audience Surveys and Interviews: Engage directly with your audience through surveys, interviews, or focus groups to gather insights into their needs, interests, and preferences. Ask open-ended questions to uncover valuable information.

b) Monitor Social Media Conversations: Pay attention to conversations happening on social media platforms related to your industry, niche, or brand. Analyse the topics, trends, and sentiments expressed by your audience to identify common themes and interests.

c) Review Customer Feedback and Reviews: Review feedback from customer reviews, testimonials, and support inquiries to understand what matters most to your audience. Look for recurring themes or areas of improvement that you can address through your community engagement efforts.

## C. Segmenting Your Community for Personalised Engagement

Not all community members are the same, so it's essential to segment your audience based on relevant criteria to personalise your engagement efforts. Here's how to segment your community effectively:

a) Demographic Segmentation: Segment your audience based on demographic factors such as age, gender, location, income, or occupation. This can help you tailor your messaging and content to resonate with specific demographic groups.

b) Psychographic Segmentation: Consider segmenting your audience based on psychographic factors such as interests, values, attitudes, or lifestyle preferences. This can help you create content and experiences that align with your audience's beliefs and motivations.

c) Behavioural Segmentation: Segment your audience based on their behaviours, such as past purchase history, engagement with your brand, or frequency of interaction. This can help you identify high-value segments and target them with relevant offers or content.

By identifying and defining your target community, analysing their needs, interests, and behaviours, and segmenting your community for personalised engagement, you can lay the foundation for effective community engagement efforts. This understanding will inform your content strategy, messaging, and interaction tactics, helping you build stronger relationships with your audience.

## III. Building and Nurturing Community Relationships

### A. Establishing Trust and Credibility

Building trust and credibility within your community is essential for fostering strong relationships and driving engagement. Here's how to establish trust and credibility:

a) Authenticity: Be authentic and transparent in your communications and interactions with community members. Share behind-the-scenes insights, stories, and updates to humanise your brand and build rapport.

b) Consistency: Consistency instils trust. Ensure that your messaging, tone, and actions are consistent across all touchpoints and interactions. Consistent branding and communication help reinforce your credibility and reliability.

c) Provide Value: Demonstrate your expertise and value to your community by offering helpful resources, insights, and solutions to their problems. Position yourself as a trusted advisor and resource within your niche or industry.

## B. Creating Valuable Content for Community Members

Creating valuable content is key to engaging and retaining community members. Here's how to create content that resonates with your audience:

a) Understand Audience Needs: Continuously listen to your community to understand their needs, challenges, and interests. Use this insight to create content that addresses their pain points and provides valuable solutions.

b) Educational Content: Provide educational content that empowers your community members to learn and grow in their areas of interest. Share tutorials, guides, how-to articles, and industry insights to add value to their lives.

c) Entertaining Content: Don't forget to entertain your audience. Create content that entertains, inspires, or sparks joy. Use humour, storytelling, or visual elements to capture attention and keep your audience engaged.

## C. Encouraging Participation and Interaction

Encouraging participation and interaction is crucial for building a vibrant and engaged community. Here's how to foster participation and interaction:

a) Ask Questions: Encourage dialogue and conversation by asking questions and soliciting feedback from your community. Use polls, surveys, or open-ended prompts to invite participation and spark discussions.

b) Facilitate Engagement: Create opportunities for community members to engage with each other and with your brand. Host live Q&A sessions, webinars, or virtual events where members can connect, share ideas, and learn from each other.

c) Recognise and Reward Engagement: Recognise and reward community members for their contributions and engagement. Highlight user-generated content, showcase member achievements, or offer exclusive perks or rewards for active participation.

By establishing trust and credibility, creating valuable content, and encouraging participation and interaction, you can cultivate a thriving community around your brand. These efforts will help strengthen relationships, drive engagement, and foster a sense of belonging among community members, ultimately leading to greater loyalty and advocacy for your brand.

## IV. Leveraging Community Platforms and Tools

### A. Choosing the Right Community Platforms (e.g., social media, forums, online groups)

Selecting the appropriate community platforms is crucial for reaching and engaging with your target audience effectively. Consider the following factors when choosing community platforms:

a) Audience Preferences: Identify where your target audience spends their time online. Research their preferred platforms, whether it's social media networks like Facebook, Twitter, or LinkedIn, forums, or specialised online groups.

b) Platform Features: Evaluate the features and functionalities of different platforms to determine which align best with your community engagement goals. Consider factors such as ease of use, Customisation options, and integration capabilities.

c) Community Size and Activity: Assess the size and activity level of existing communities on each platform. Choose platforms where your target audience is actively engaged and where there is potential for growth and interaction.

d) Moderation and Safety: Consider the moderation and safety features offered by each platform. Ensure that the platform provides adequate tools for managing and moderating discussions, protecting user privacy, and maintaining a positive and inclusive community environment.

## B. Implementing Community Management Best Practices

Effective community management is essential for fostering a positive and engaging community environment. Here are some best practices for community management:

a) Establish Clear Guidelines: Develop clear community guidelines outlining expected behaviours, rules, and norms for participation. Communicate these guidelines to community members and enforce them consistently to maintain order and civility.

b) Be Responsive and Engaging: Be responsive to community members' questions, comments, and concerns. Foster two-way communication by actively engaging with members, responding to inquiries, and acknowledging feedback promptly.

c) Empower Community Leaders: Identify and empower community leaders or moderators to help manage discussions, resolve conflicts, and enforce community guidelines. Provide training and support to equip them with the tools and resources they need to succeed.

d) Encourage Positive Interactions: Foster a culture of positivity and respect within the community. Encourage members to support and uplift each other, celebrate achievements, and provide constructive feedback in a respectful manner.

## C. Utilising Community Engagement Tools and Analytics

Community engagement tools and analytics can provide valuable insights into community dynamics, member behaviour, and content performance. Here's how to utilise these tools effectively:

a) Engagement Tracking: Use engagement tracking tools to monitor community activity, track member participation, and identify trends in engagement levels over time. Analyse metrics such as likes, comments, shares, and interactions to gauge the health of your community.

b) Sentiment Analysis: Employ sentiment analysis tools to analyse member sentiment and identify patterns in sentiment trends. Monitor sentiment indicators to assess community sentiment and sentiment shifts in response to different events or topics.

c) Content Performance Analysis: Use analytics tools to track the performance of your content within the community. Measure metrics such as reach, engagement, and conversion rates to evaluate the effectiveness of your content strategy and identify areas for improvement.

d) Community Feedback Surveys: Conduct regular community feedback surveys to gather insights into member satisfaction, preferences, and needs. Use survey results to inform community management strategies, content planning, and platform improvements.

By choosing the right community platforms, implementing community management best practices, and utilising community engagement tools and analytics effectively, you can create a thriving and engaged community around your brand. These efforts will help you build stronger relationships with your audience, drive meaningful interactions, and achieve your community engagement goals.

## V. Measuring and Analysing Community Engagement

## A. Key Metrics for Evaluating Community Engagement

Measuring community engagement is essential for understanding the effectiveness of your community-building efforts. Here are key metrics to consider:

a) Membership Growth: Track the growth of your community over time to assess its popularity and reach.

b) Active Membership: Monitor the number of active members who regularly participate in discussions, share content, or interact with other members.

c) Engagement Rate: Calculate the engagement rate by dividing the number of engagements (likes, comments, shares) by the total number of community members. This metric indicates the level of interaction and participation within the community.

d) Response Time: Measure the average response time to member inquiries or comments to gauge the responsiveness of your community management team.

e) Content Performance: Analyse the performance of community-generated content, such as posts, discussions, or user-generated content. Track metrics like views, likes, comments, and shares to identify popular topics and trends.

## B. Analytics Tools and Platforms for Community Analysis

Utilise analytics tools and platforms to gather data and insights about your community. Here are some tools and platforms to consider:

a) Google Analytics: Use Google Analytics to track website traffic, user behaviour, and engagement metrics. Set up custom reports to monitor community-related metrics and user interactions on your website or blog.

b) Social Media Analytics: Most social media platforms offer built-in analytics tools that provide insights into audience demographics, engagement metrics, and content performance. Platforms like Facebook Insights, Twitter Analytics, and LinkedIn Analytics offer valuable data for analysing community engagement.

c) Community Management Platforms: Consider using community management platforms like Hootsuite, Sprout Social, or HubSpot to manage and analyse your community across multiple channels. These platforms offer features for scheduling posts, monitoring mentions, and analysing engagement metrics.

d) Survey and Feedback Tools: Use survey and feedback tools like SurveyMonkey, Typeform, or Google Forms to gather feedback from community members. Conduct regular surveys to assess member satisfaction, preferences, and needs.

C. Continuous Monitoring and Adaptation Strategies

Continuous monitoring and adaptation are key to maintaining a healthy and engaged community. Here are strategies to consider:

a) Regular Monitoring: Monitor community engagement metrics regularly to track performance trends and identify areas for improvement.

b) Feedback Loop: Establish a feedback loop with community members to gather input, suggestions, and feedback on community initiatives and activities. Use this feedback to make data-driven decisions and adapt your strategy accordingly.

c) A/B Testing: Conduct A/B tests to experiment with different community engagement tactics, content formats, or messaging strategies. Measure the impact of these tests on engagement metrics and adjust your approach based on the results.

d) Iterative Improvement: Implement a process of iterative improvement, where you continuously test, learn, and refine your community engagement strategies based on data and insights.

By evaluating key metrics for community engagement, leveraging analytics tools and platforms, and implementing continuous monitoring and adaptation strategies, you can effectively measure, analyse, and optimise your community engagement efforts. This iterative approach will help you build a vibrant and engaged community that fosters meaningful connections and drives positive outcomes for your brand.

## VI. Cultivating a Culture of Engagement

### A. Encouraging User-Generated Content and Contributions

User-generated content (UGC) is a powerful tool for building community engagement and fostering a sense of ownership among your audience. Here's how to encourage UGC and contributions:

a) Create Opportunities for Participation: Provide clear prompts, challenges, or calls to action that encourage community members to contribute their own content. Whether it's through contests, challenges, or themed campaigns, make it easy for members to participate and share their creations.

b) Highlight User Contributions: Showcase user-generated content prominently within your community to Recognise and celebrate member contributions. Feature user stories, testimonials, or creative works to inspire others and reinforce the value of participation.

c) Offer Incentives and Rewards: Encourage participation by offering incentives or rewards for user-generated content. Whether it's through prizes, recognition, or exclusive perks, provide tangible benefits to motivate members to contribute and engage.

## B. Facilitating Meaningful Discussions and Interactions

Meaningful discussions and interactions are the lifeblood of a vibrant community. Here's how to facilitate meaningful interactions:

a) Set the Tone: Establish a positive and inclusive tone within your community to foster open dialogue and respectful interactions. Encourage members to share their thoughts, opinions, and experiences in a supportive environment.

b) Ask Thought-Provoking Questions: Stimulate conversation by asking thought-provoking questions that spark discussion and debate. Encourage members to share their insights, perspectives, and personal experiences on relevant topics.

c) Provide Resources and Information: Share valuable resources, articles, or expert insights to fuel discussions and provide context for conversation. Offer educational content that empowers members to learn and grow within the community.

## C. Empowering Community Advocates and Brand Ambassadors

Empowering community advocates and brand ambassadors is essential for driving engagement and advocacy. Here's how to empower your most passionate supporters:

a) Identify and Recognise Advocates: Identify community members who consistently contribute valuable insights, support others, or advocate for your brand. Recognise and celebrate their efforts publicly to reinforce their importance within the community.

b) Provide Opportunities for Leadership: Empower advocates to take on leadership roles within the community, such as moderators, mentors, or ambassadors. Give them a platform to share their expertise, lead discussions, and drive positive change.

c) Offer Exclusive Benefits: Provide exclusive benefits or perks to community advocates, such as early access to new products, VIP events, or special discounts. Reward their loyalty and advocacy with tangible incentives that demonstrate your appreciation.

By encouraging user-generated content and contributions, facilitating meaningful discussions and interactions, and empowering community advocates and brand ambassadors, you can create a dynamic and engaged community that fosters connection, collaboration, and advocacy. These efforts will help strengthen relationships, drive positive word-of-mouth, and elevate your brand's reputation and influence within the community.

## VII. Case Studies and Examples of Successful Community Engagement

### A. Real-World Examples of Brands Fostering Community Engagement

*Lululemon*

Lululemon, a popular athletic apparel brand, has built a strong community around its brand by hosting free yoga classes, running clubs, and other fitness events in its stores. These events not only provide value to customers but also create opportunities for like-minded individuals to connect and engage with the brand in a meaningful way.

*LEGO*

LEGO has cultivated a vibrant online community through its LEGO Ideas platform, where fans can submit their own designs for new LEGO sets. Community members can vote on their favourite designs, and those that receive enough support may be turned into official LEGO products. This crowdsourcing approach not only fosters creativity and collaboration but also empowers fans to play a role in shaping the brand's product offerings.

*Airbnb*

Airbnb has built a community of hosts and guests by facilitating connections and interactions between users. Through features like host profiles, guest reviews, and community forums, Airbnb encourages trust, communication, and collaboration among its members. This sense of community not only enhances the user experience but also contributes to the overall success of the platform.

B. Lessons Learned and Best Practices from Community Engagement Success Stories

Focus on Value Creation: Successful community engagement efforts are rooted in creating value for members. Whether it's through educational content, networking opportunities, or exclusive benefits, prioritise providing value to your community to keep members engaged and invested in the community.

*Authenticity and Transparency*

Authenticity and transparency are essential for building trust and credibility within your community. Be genuine in your interactions, communicate openly with members, and be transparent about your brand values, goals, and initiatives.

*Empowerment and Participation*

Empower community members to actively participate and contribute to the community. Provide opportunities for members to share their insights, ideas, and experiences, and recognise and reward their contributions to foster a sense of ownership and belonging.

*Listen and Adapt*

Listen to feedback from your community and be willing to adapt and evolve based on their needs and preferences. Pay attention to trends, sentiment, and engagement metrics, and use this data to inform your community engagement strategies and initiatives.

By studying real-world examples of brands fostering community engagement and extracting lessons learned and best practices, you can gain valuable insights into how to effectively build and nurture a thriving community around your brand. Implementing these strategies and principles can help you create a dynamic and engaged community that drives positive outcomes for your brand and its members.

## VIII. Conclusion: Building Stronger Community Connections

### A. Recap of Key Insights and Strategies

Throughout this chapter, we've explored the importance of community engagement and strategies for fostering meaningful connections with your audience. Here's a recap of key insights and strategies:

a) Encouraging User-Generated Content: Empower your community members to contribute their own content and creations, fostering a sense of ownership and pride within the community.

b) Facilitating Meaningful Discussions: Create opportunities for meaningful interactions and dialogue among community members, stimulating engagement and collaboration.

c) Empowering Advocates: Recognise and empower community advocates and brand ambassadors, leveraging their enthusiasm and passion to amplify your brand's message and influence.

d) Choosing the Right Platforms: Select community platforms that align with your audience's preferences and behaviours, maximising your reach and engagement potential.

e) Continuous Monitoring and Adaptation: Continuously monitor community engagement metrics and adapt your strategies based on feedback and insights, ensuring ongoing relevance and effectiveness.

B. Encouragement for Implementing Community Engagement Tactics

Now that you're equipped with the knowledge and strategies for effective community engagement, it's time to put them into action. Don't be afraid to experiment, iterate, and refine your approach as you build and nurture your community. Remember, building strong community connections takes time and effort, but the rewards are well worth it.

C. Looking Ahead to Building Stronger Community Connections

As you look ahead, focus on building even stronger community connections by deepening relationships, expanding your reach, and fostering a culture of collaboration and support. Continue to listen to your community, adapt to their evolving needs, and innovate new ways to engage and delight them. By prioritising community engagement and investing in meaningful connections, you'll not only strengthen your brand's relationship with its audience but also create a loyal and dedicated community that advocates for your brand and drives its success.

# Chapter 6: Measuring and Analysing Engagement

## I. Introduction to Measuring Engagement

### A. Importance of Measuring Engagement

Measuring engagement is paramount in assessing the effectiveness of content marketing strategies and understanding audience interactions with your brand. Here's why measuring engagement matters:

a) Performance Evaluation: Engagement metrics provide valuable insights into how well your content resonates with your audience. By tracking engagement, you can evaluate the success of your content initiatives and identify areas for improvement.

b) Audience Understanding: Engagement metrics offer a window into audience behaviour, preferences, and interests. Analysing engagement data helps you gain a deeper understanding of your audience, allowing you to tailor your content to better meet their needs.

c) Optimisation Opportunities: Measuring engagement enables you to optimise your content marketing efforts for better results. By identifying high-performing content and understanding what drives audience engagement, you can refine your strategies to maximise impact and ROI.

d) Decision Making: Engagement data serves as a guide for making informed decisions about content creation, distribution channels, and audience targeting. It provides evidence-based insights that inform strategic planning and resource allocation.

### B. Overview of Chapter Objectives

In this chapter, we'll delve into the various aspects of measuring and analysing engagement in content marketing. Our objectives include:

a) Understanding Engagement Metrics: We'll explore the different types of engagement metrics and their significance in evaluating audience interactions with content.

b) Exploring Analytics Tools: We'll discuss the tools and platforms available for measuring engagement, from web analytics to social media monitoring tools.

c) Setting Up Measurement Frameworks: We'll provide guidance on establishing measurement frameworks, including goal setting, KPI definition, and tracking implementation.

d) Interpreting and Analysing Data: We'll cover techniques for interpreting and analysing engagement data, including data visualisation, trend identification, and audience behaviour analysis.

e) Continuous Monitoring and Adaptation: We'll emphasise the importance of ongoing analysis and adaptation, highlighting strategies for iterative optimisation and adaptation to changing trends.

By the end of this chapter, you'll have a comprehensive understanding of how to effectively measure and analyse engagement in content marketing, empowering you to make data-driven decisions and optimise your strategies for improved audience engagement and business outcomes.

## II. Key Metrics for Evaluating Engagement

### A. Definition and Significance of Engagement Metrics

Engagement metrics encompass a range of measurements that gauge how actively and deeply your audience interacts with your content and brand. Understanding the significance of engagement metrics is essential for evaluating the effectiveness of your content marketing efforts. Here's why engagement metrics matter:

a) Indicator of Audience Interest: Engagement metrics provide insights into the level of interest and attention your audience has towards your content. Metrics such as likes, comments, shares, and time spent on page indicate the extent to which your content resonates with your audience.

b) Measure of Content Effectiveness: Engagement metrics serve as a barometer for assessing the effectiveness of your content in capturing and retaining audience attention. By tracking engagement metrics, you can identify which content performs well and which needs improvement, enabling you to refine your content strategy accordingly.

c) Driver of Audience Interaction: Engaging content is more likely to elicit actions and responses from your audience, such as sharing, commenting, or clicking through to your website. Engagement metrics reflect the level of interaction and participation generated by your content, helping you gauge its impact on audience behaviour.

d) Indicator of Brand Affinity: High levels of engagement signal a strong connection between your audience and your brand. When audiences actively engage with your content, it indicates a positive perception of your brand and a willingness to interact and engage further.

B. Types of Engagement Metrics

Engagement metrics can be categorised into three main types, each providing valuable insights into different aspects of audience interaction and behaviour:

*Audience Engagement Metrics*

Audience engagement metrics focus on how actively your audience interacts with your content and brand across various channels. Key audience engagement metrics include:

a) Likes: The number of likes or reactions your content receives on social media platforms.

b) Comments: The number of comments or replies generated by your content, indicating audience feedback and interaction.

c) Shares: The number of times your content is shared with others, extending its reach and visibility.

d) Followers/Subscribers: The size and growth of your audience base, indicating the level of interest in your brand and content.

*Content Engagement Metrics*

Content engagement metrics assess how effectively your content captures and retains audience attention. Key content engagement metrics include:

a) Page Views: The number of times your content is viewed or accessed by users, indicating its popularity and reach.

b) Time Spent on Page: The average duration users spend consuming your content, reflecting its level of interest and engagement.

c) Bounce Rate: The percentage of visitors who navigate away from your site after viewing only one page, indicating the relevance and engagement of your content.

*Conversion and Action Metrics*

Conversion and action metrics measure the effectiveness of your content in driving desired outcomes and actions from your audience. Key conversion and action metrics include:

a) Click-Through Rate (CTR): The percentage of users who click on a specific link or call-to-action (CTA) within your content, indicating its effectiveness in driving traffic and engagement.
b) Conversion Rate: The percentage of users who complete a desired action, such as making a purchase or signing up for a newsletter, as a result of interacting with your content.

c) Goal Completions: The number of times users complete predefined goals or actions on your website, such as form submissions, downloads, or purchases, indicating the success of your content in achieving business objectives.

By understanding the different types of engagement metrics and their significance, you can effectively measure and evaluate the impact of your content marketing efforts on audience engagement, behaviour, and business outcomes.

## III. Analytics Tools and Platforms

### A. Google Analytics

Google Analytics is a powerful web analytics tool that provides comprehensive insights into website traffic, user behaviour, and engagement metrics. Key features and capabilities of Google Analytics include:

a) Audience Insights: Google Analytics allows you to understand your website visitors better by providing demographic information, such as age, gender, and location. You can also analyse user interests and behaviour, including new vs. returning visitors and user engagement metrics.

b) Traffic Sources Analysis: With Google Analytics, you can track the sources of your website traffic, including organic search, paid search, social media, direct traffic, and referral traffic. This helps you identify which channels drive the most visitors to your site and optimise your marketing efforts accordingly.

c) Content Performance: Google Analytics provides detailed insights into the performance of your website content, including page views, time spent on page, bounce rate, and exit rate. You can analyse the effectiveness of individual pages, blog posts, and content categories to identify high-performing content and areas for improvement.

d) Conversion Tracking: Google Analytics allows you to set up conversion tracking to measure specific actions or goals on your website, such as form submissions, purchases, or newsletter sign-ups. You can track conversions, analyse conversion funnels, and optimise your website for better conversion rates.

## B. Social Media Analytics

Social media analytics tools provide insights into the performance and effectiveness of your social media marketing efforts across various platforms. Key features of social media analytics tools include:

a) Audience Demographics: Social media analytics tools allow you to analyse the demographics of your social media followers, including age, gender, location, and interests. This helps you understand your audience better and tailor your content to their preferences.

b) Engagement Metrics: Social media analytics tools provide metrics such as likes, comments, shares, retweets, and mentions, which measure the level of engagement with your social media content. You can track engagement trends over time, identify popular content, and optimise your social media strategy for better engagement.

c) Reach and Impressions: Social media analytics tools allow you to track the reach and impressions of your social media posts, indicating how many users have seen your content. You can analyse reach and impressions by post type, time of day, and audience demographics to optimise your posting strategy for maximum visibility.

d) Competitor Analysis: Some social media analytics tools offer competitive analysis features that allow you to benchmark your performance against competitors. You can compare metrics such as follower growth, engagement rate, and content performance to identify opportunities and areas for improvement.

C. Content Management Systems (CMS)

Content Management Systems (CMS) provide tools and functionalities for creating, managing, and publishing digital content. Key features of CMS platforms include:

a) Content Creation and Editing: CMS platforms allow you to create and edit content easily using a user-friendly interface. You can create various types of content, including blog posts, articles, videos, and images, and organise them into categories or topics.

b) Content Publishing: CMS platforms streamline the process of publishing content by providing scheduling and automation features. You can schedule content to be published at specific times, set up automated publishing workflows, and manage content publication across multiple channels.

c) Content Performance Tracking: Some CMS platforms offer built-in analytics and reporting tools that allow you to track the performance of your content. You can monitor metrics such as page views, engagement, and conversion rates directly within the CMS dashboard, enabling you to optimise your content strategy in real-time.

d) SEO Optimisation: Many CMS platforms include SEO optimisation features that help improve the visibility and searchability of your content. You can optimise content for target keywords, meta tags, and other SEO elements directly within the CMS, ensuring that your content ranks well in search engine results.

## D. Email Marketing Platforms

Email marketing platforms are tools that enable businesses to create, send, and track email marketing campaigns. Key features of email marketing platforms include:

a) Email Campaign Creation: Email marketing platforms provide templates and drag-and-drop editors for creating visually appealing email campaigns. You can customise email templates, add images and multimedia content, and personalise messages for your audience.

b) List Management: Email marketing platforms allow you to manage your email subscriber lists effectively. You can segment your audience based on demographics, interests, or behaviour, and target them with relevant and personalised email content.

c) Campaign Automation: Email marketing platforms offer automation features that enable you to automate email workflows and sequences. You can set up triggered emails based on user actions or schedule automated email campaigns to nurture leads, onboard new subscribers, or re-engage inactive users.

d) Performance Tracking: Email marketing platforms provide analytics and reporting tools that allow you to track the performance of your email campaigns. You can monitor metrics such as open rates, click-through rates, conversion rates, and unsubscribe rates to measure the effectiveness of your email marketing efforts.

## E. Customer Relationship Management (CRM) Systems

Customer Relationship Management (CRM) systems are software platforms that help businesses manage customer relationships, sales pipelines, and marketing campaigns. Key features of CRM systems include:

a) Contact Management: CRM systems centralise customer data and provide tools for managing contact information, communication history, and customer interactions. You can track customer interactions across multiple channels, including email, phone calls, social media, and website visits.

b) Sales Pipeline Management: CRM systems enable you to track and manage sales opportunities through the entire sales pipeline. You can track leads, opportunities, and deals, assign tasks to sales reps, and monitor sales performance in real-time.

c) Marketing Automation Integration: Many CRM systems integrate with marketing automation platforms to streamline lead generation and nurturing processes. You can capture leads from various sources, automate lead scoring and segmentation, and execute targeted marketing campaigns based on CRM data.

d) Analytics and Reporting: CRM systems offer analytics and reporting features that provide insights into customer behaviour, sales performance, and marketing effectiveness. You can generate custom reports, dashboards, and visualisations to track key metrics and make data-driven decisions.

By leveraging these analytics tools and platforms, businesses can gain valuable insights into audience behaviour, content performance, and marketing effectiveness, enabling them to optimise their strategies for better results and ROI.

## IV. Setting Up Measurement Frameworks

### A. Establishing Goals and Objectives

Before diving into measuring engagement, it's essential to establish clear goals and objectives for your content marketing efforts. Here's how to get started:

a) Define Your Objectives: Start by identifying what you want to achieve with your content marketing strategy. Are you aiming to increase brand awareness, drive website traffic, generate leads, or boost sales? Clearly define your objectives to align your measurement efforts with your overarching business goals.

b) Set SMART Goals: Make sure your goals are Specific, Measurable, Achievable, Relevant, and Time-bound (SMART). For example, instead of setting a vague goal like "increase website traffic," set a specific target, such as "increase website traffic by 20% in the next six months."

c) Consider Audience Needs: Take into account the needs and preferences of your target audience when setting goals. Your content should aim to provide value and address audience pain points to drive engagement and conversions.

## B. Defining Key Performance Indicators (KPIs)

Once you've established your goals, it's time to identify the key performance indicators (KPIs) that will help you track progress towards those goals. Here's how to define KPIs effectively:

a) Align KPIs with Goals: Each goal should have corresponding KPIs that directly measure progress towards that goal. For example, if your goal is to increase brand awareness, relevant KPIs might include social media reach, website traffic, or brand mentions.

b) Focus on Metrics that Matter: Avoid tracking vanity metrics that don't provide meaningful insights into your performance. Instead, prioritise KPIs that align with your objectives and have a direct impact on business outcomes.

c) Choose Quantifiable Metrics: Ensure that your KPIs are quantifiable and measurable. This allows you to track progress over time and evaluate the effectiveness of your content marketing efforts accurately.

### C. Implementing Tracking and Tagging

Once you've identified your goals and KPIs, it's crucial to implement tracking and tagging mechanisms to measure and analyse relevant data. Here's how to implement tracking and tagging effectively:

a) Utilise Analytics Tools: Leverage analytics tools such as Google Analytics, social media analytics platforms, and email marketing platforms to track and measure engagement metrics. Set up tracking codes, tags, and pixels to capture relevant data from your digital properties.

b) Customise Tracking Parameters: Configure tracking parameters and events based on your specific goals and KPIs. For example, set up goal conversions, event tracking, and custom dimensions in Google Analytics to capture data relevant to your objectives.

c) Regularly Monitor and Analyse Data: Continuously monitor and analyse the data collected from tracking and tagging efforts. Use dashboards, reports, and data visualisation tools to gain insights into audience behaviour, content performance, and campaign effectiveness.

By establishing clear goals and objectives, defining relevant KPIs, and implementing effective tracking and tagging mechanisms, you can create a robust measurement framework that enables you to evaluate the success of your content marketing efforts and make data-driven decisions to optimise performance.

## V. Interpreting and Analysing Data

### A. Data Visualisation Techniques

Data visualisation techniques play a crucial role in transforming complex data sets into actionable insights that are easy to understand and interpret. Here are some effective data visualisation techniques:

a) Charts and Graphs: Utilise various types of charts and graphs, such as line charts, bar charts, pie charts, and scatter plots, to visualise trends, comparisons, and distributions in your data. Choose the most appropriate chart type based on the nature of your data and the insights you want to convey.

b) Dashboards: Create interactive dashboards that consolidate key metrics and performance indicators in a single view. Dashboards allow stakeholders to quickly assess performance, track progress towards goals, and identify areas that require attention.

c) Heatmaps: Use heatmaps to visualise patterns of user behaviour on your website or digital platform. Heatmaps provide insights into where users are clicking, scrolling, and spending the most time, helping you optimise user experience and content placement.

d) Word Clouds: Generate word clouds to visually represent the frequency of terms or keywords within a text-based dataset. Word clouds make it easy to identify common themes, topics, or trends in qualitative data, such as customer feedback or social media comments.

## B. Identifying Trends and Patterns

Identifying trends and patterns in your data allows you to uncover valuable insights and make informed decisions about your content marketing strategy. Here's how to effectively identify trends and patterns:

a) Time-Series Analysis: Analyse data over time to identify long-term trends, seasonal patterns, and recurring cycles. Use line charts or time-series plots to visualise changes in key metrics over different time periods and identify patterns of growth or decline.

b) Segmentation Analysis: Segment your data based on relevant variables, such as demographics, geography, or behaviour, to identify patterns and trends within specific audience segments. Compare performance metrics across segments to understand differences in audience preferences and behaviour.

c) Correlation Analysis: Explore relationships between different variables in your data to uncover correlations and dependencies. Identify factors that are strongly correlated with key performance indicators to understand what drives engagement and conversion.

d) Forecasting: Use statistical techniques and forecasting models to predict future trends and anticipate changes in audience behaviour. By analysing historical data and extrapolating trends, you can make proactive decisions and adjust your content marketing strategy accordingly.

## C. Understanding Audience Behaviour

Understanding audience behaviour is essential for crafting targeted content and delivering personalised experiences that resonate with your audience. Here's how to gain insights into audience behaviour:

a) User Journey Analysis: Analyse the typical user journey or path that visitors take on your website or digital platform. Identify common touchpoints, interactions, and conversion paths to optimise user experience and content engagement.

b) Behavioural Segmentation: Segment your audience based on behavioural attributes, such as browsing behaviour, purchase history, or engagement level. Identify distinct audience segments and tailor your content and messaging to address their specific needs and preferences.

c) Content Interaction Analysis: Track how users interact with your content, including page views, time spent on page, scroll depth, and click-through rates. Analyse content performance metrics to identify high-performing content, popular topics, and areas for improvement.

d) Feedback Analysis: Collect and analyse feedback from your audience through surveys, polls, comments, and social media mentions. Pay attention to sentiment, common themes, and suggestions for improvement to gain insights into audience preferences and sentiment.

By leveraging data visualisation techniques, identifying trends and patterns, and understanding audience behaviour, you can gain valuable insights into the effectiveness of your content marketing efforts and make data-driven decisions to optimise performance and achieve your business objectives.

## VI. Continuous Monitoring and Adaptation

### A. Importance of Ongoing Analysis

Ongoing analysis is crucial for maintaining the effectiveness of your content marketing strategies over time. Here's why continuous monitoring and analysis are essential:

a) Performance Evaluation: Regular analysis allows you to assess the performance of your content marketing efforts and identify areas of success and improvement. By monitoring key metrics and KPIs, you can track progress towards your goals and make data-driven decisions to optimise performance.

b) Insight Generation: Ongoing analysis generates valuable insights into audience behaviour, content effectiveness, and market trends. By analysing data trends, patterns, and audience feedback, you can uncover new opportunities, identify emerging trends, and adapt your strategies accordingly.

c) Optimisation Opportunities: Continuous analysis enables you to identify optimisation opportunities and refine your content marketing strategies for better results. By experimenting with different tactics, iterating on successful approaches, and learning from failures, you can continuously improve your content and tactics to drive engagement and conversions.

## B. Iterative Optimisation Strategies

Iterative optimisation involves testing, measuring, and refining your content marketing strategies over time. Here's how to implement iterative optimisation strategies effectively:

a) A/B Testing: A/B testing involves comparing two versions of a piece of content, such as email subject lines, landing pages, or ad creatives, to determine which performs better. By testing different variables and measuring the results, you can identify the most effective strategies and optimise your content for maximum impact.

b) Data-Driven Decision Making: Base your optimisation decisions on data and insights rather than assumptions or gut feelings. Use analytics tools and performance metrics to evaluate the effectiveness of your content marketing efforts and guide your optimisation efforts.

c) Continuous Improvement: Embrace a mindset of continuous improvement and experimentation. Regularly review performance data, test new ideas, and iterate on successful tactics to stay ahead of the curve and drive ongoing growth and success.

## C. Adaptation to Changing Trends

The digital landscape is constantly evolving, with new technologies, platforms, and trends emerging regularly. Here's how to adapt your content marketing strategies to changing trends:

a) Stay Informed: Stay informed about industry trends, market changes, and emerging technologies that may impact your content marketing strategies. Follow industry blogs, attend conferences, and engage with thought leaders to stay up to date on the latest developments.

b) Monitor Audience Behaviour: Monitor changes in audience behaviour, preferences, and consumption patterns to identify shifts in trends and adapt your content strategies accordingly. Pay attention to changes in search behaviour, social media usage, and content consumption habits to stay relevant and meet evolving audience needs.

c) Flexibility and Agility: Maintain flexibility and agility in your content marketing approach to quickly respond to changing trends and market conditions. Be willing to experiment with new formats, channels, and tactics, and adjust your strategies based on feedback and performance data.

By prioritising ongoing analysis, embracing iterative optimisation strategies, and adapting to changing trends, you can ensure the long-term success and effectiveness of your content marketing efforts in an ever-evolving digital landscape.

## VII. Real-World Measurement Practices

### A. Real-World Examples of Effective Measurement Practices

*HubSpot's Inbound Marketing Metrics*

HubSpot, a leading inbound marketing platform, emphasises the importance of measuring key inbound marketing metrics such as website traffic, leads generated, and customer acquisition costs. By tracking these metrics, HubSpot can assess the effectiveness of its content marketing efforts and make data-driven decisions to optimise performance.

*Red Bull's Content Engagement Metrics*

Red Bull, known for its innovative content marketing initiatives, closely monitors engagement metrics such as views, likes, shares, and comments across its various content channels, including social media, YouTube, and its website. By analysing these engagement metrics, Red Bull can gauge audience interest and preferences, identify high-performing content, and tailor its content strategy to maximise engagement.

*Airbnb's Conversion Tracking*

Airbnb, a global online marketplace for lodging and tourism experiences, utilises advanced conversion tracking techniques to measure the impact of its content marketing efforts on user bookings and revenue generation. By tracking conversions at each stage of the user journey, from initial website visit to booking confirmation, Airbnb can attribute conversions to specific content interactions and optimise its content strategy for higher conversion rates.

### B. Lessons Learned and Best Practices from Success Stories

a) Focus on Relevant Metrics: Successful organisations prioritise measuring metrics that directly align with their business goals and objectives. By focusing on relevant metrics such as lead generation, customer acquisition, and revenue attribution, businesses can ensure that their measurement efforts provide actionable insights and drive tangible results.

b) Iterative Optimisation: Success stories emphasise the importance of iterative optimisation, where organisations continuously test, measure, and refine their content marketing strategies based on performance data and audience feedback. By embracing a culture of experimentation and learning, businesses can adapt to changing market conditions and stay ahead of the competition.

c) Data-Driven Decision Making: Leading organisations leverage data-driven decision-making processes to inform their content marketing strategies and tactics. By analysing performance data, identifying trends and patterns, and deriving actionable insights, businesses can make informed decisions that drive meaningful outcomes and deliver measurable ROI.

d) Continuous Improvement: Success stories highlight the value of continuous improvement in content marketing practices. By constantly seeking ways to enhance content quality, optimise distribution channels, and improve audience engagement, businesses can maintain a competitive edge and drive sustained growth in a dynamic and evolving digital landscape.

By studying real-world examples of effective measurement practices and drawing lessons from success stories, businesses can gain valuable insights and inspiration for optimising their own content marketing strategies and achieving greater success in engaging audiences and driving business results.

## VIII. Conclusion: Maximising Engagement through Effective Measurement

### A. Recap of Key Insights and Strategies

Throughout this chapter, we've explored the importance of ongoing analysis, iterative optimisation, and adaptation to changing trends in maximising engagement through effective measurement. Key insights and strategies include:

a) The significance of continuous monitoring and analysis to assess content marketing performance and uncover actionable insights.

b) The value of iterative optimisation strategies such as A/B testing, data-driven decision making, and continuous improvement in driving meaningful outcomes.

c) The importance of adaptation to changing trends and market conditions to stay relevant and meet evolving audience needs.

## B. Encouragement for Implementing Measurement Tactics

Implementing measurement tactics can seem daunting, but it's essential for unlocking the full potential of your content marketing efforts. Here's why you should embrace measurement tactics:

a) Measurement provides valuable feedback on the effectiveness of your content marketing strategies, helping you identify areas for improvement and optimisation.

b) By implementing measurement tactics, you can make informed decisions based on data and insights rather than assumptions or guesswork.

c) Measurement allows you to demonstrate the ROI of your content marketing efforts and justify investment in future initiatives.

## C. Looking Ahead to Enhanced Engagement Strategies

As you continue your content marketing journey, it's essential to look ahead to enhanced engagement strategies that build upon your measurement efforts. Here's what the future holds:

a) Embrace emerging technologies and trends such as artificial intelligence, interactive content, and immersive experiences to captivate and engage your audience.

b) Foster deeper connections with your audience through personalised content experiences tailored to their preferences, interests, and needs.

c) Cultivate a culture of experimentation and innovation, where continuous learning and adaptation drive ongoing growth and success.

By implementing measurement tactics, embracing emerging engagement strategies, and staying agile in the face of change, you can maximise engagement and drive meaningful outcomes in your content marketing efforts. Remember, effective measurement is not just about tracking numbers—it's about leveraging insights to create more engaging and impactful experiences for your audience.

# Chapter 7: Personalisation in Content Marketing

## I. Introduction to Personalisation

### A. Audience Segmentation and Profiling

Audience segmentation involves dividing your audience into smaller, more manageable groups based on shared characteristics, preferences, and behaviours. This process allows marketers to tailor their content and messaging to specific segments, increasing relevance and engagement.

- a) Understanding Audience Segmentation: Exploring demographic factors (age, gender, location), psychographic variables (interests, values, attitudes), and behavioural patterns (purchase history, website interactions).

- b) Creating Audience Profiles: Developing detailed personas that represent different segments of your audience, including their goals, pain points, and preferred content formats.

- c) Benefits of Audience Segmentation: Improved targeting, personalised messaging, and enhanced user experiences, leading to higher conversion rates and customer satisfaction.

### B. Data Collection and Analysis for Personalisation

Effective personalisation relies on robust data collection and analysis to gain insights into audience preferences and behaviours.

- a) Data Sources: Identifying and accessing relevant data sources, including first-party data (website analytics, customer surveys), second-party data (partnerships, collaborations), and third-party data (market research, social media insights).

b) Data Privacy and Compliance: Ensuring compliance with data privacy regulations (e.g., GDPR, CCPA) and adopting transparent data collection practices to build trust with users.

c) Data Analysis Techniques: Leveraging data analytics tools and methodologies (e.g., segmentation analysis, clustering algorithms) to uncover patterns, trends, and correlations within the data.

## C. Leveraging Audience Insights for Tailored Experiences

Once audience insights are gathered, marketers can leverage this information to create personalised and tailored experiences for their audience.

a) Content Customisation: Adapting content elements such as messaging, imagery, and tone to resonate with specific audience segments.

b) Dynamic Content Delivery: Implementing dynamic content delivery mechanisms to serve personalised content based on user preferences, behaviour, and context.

c) Testing and Optimisation: Continuously testing and optimising personalised experiences to improve relevance and effectiveness over time.

By understanding audience segmentation and profiling, collecting and analysing relevant data, and leveraging audience insights for tailored experiences, marketers can create more personalised and impactful content marketing campaigns that resonate with their target audience.

## II. Understanding Your Audience for Personalisation

### A. Audience Segmentation and Profiling

Audience segmentation is the process of dividing a larger target audience into smaller, more homogeneous groups based on shared characteristics, interests, and behaviours. Profiling involves creating detailed descriptions or personas for each segment to better understand their needs and preferences.

- a) Types of Segmentation: Exploring demographic factors (age, gender, location), psychographic variables (interests, values, lifestyles), and behavioural data (purchase history, website interactions).

- b) Benefits of Segmentation: Improved targeting and relevancy, increased engagement and conversion rates, and more effective communication with different audience segments.

- c) Creating Audience Personas: Developing fictional representations of typical customers within each segment, including their goals, pain points, motivations, and preferred content formats.

## B. Data Collection and Analysis for Personalisation

- a) Effective personalisation relies on collecting and analysing relevant data to gain insights into audience behaviour and preferences.

- b) Data Sources: Identifying sources of data, including first-party data (website analytics, customer surveys), second-party data (partnerships, collaborations), and third-party data (market research, social media insights).

- c) Data Privacy Considerations: Ensuring compliance with data protection regulations (e.g., GDPR, CCPA) and maintaining transparency about data collection practices to build trust with users.

- d) Analytics Tools and Techniques: Utilising data analytics tools and methodologies (e.g., segmentation analysis, predictive modelling) to extract actionable insights from collected data.

## C. Leveraging Audience Insights for Tailored Experiences

Once audience insights are gathered, marketers can use this information to create personalised and tailored experiences for their audience.

a) Content Customisation: Adapting content elements such as messaging, imagery, and tone to resonate with specific audience segments.

b) Dynamic Content Delivery: Implementing dynamic content delivery mechanisms to serve personalised content based on user preferences, behaviour, and context.

c) Testing and Optimisation: Continuously testing and optimising personalised experiences to improve relevance and effectiveness over time.

By effectively segmenting and profiling their audience, collecting and analysing relevant data, and leveraging audience insights for tailored experiences, marketers can create more personalised and impactful content marketing campaigns that resonate with their target audience.

## III Implementing Personalisation Tactics

### A. Dynamic Content Creation Techniques

a) Dynamic content creation involves the use of technology and data to deliver personalised content experiences to users based on their behaviour, preferences, and context.

b) Dynamic Content Types: Exploring various types of dynamic content, including personalised recommendations, real-time updates, and interactive elements.

c) Data-Driven Personalisation: Leveraging user data such as browsing history, past interactions, and demographics to dynamically generate content.

d) Automation and Personalisation: Implementing automation tools and algorithms to dynamically adjust content elements in real-time based on user actions and preferences.

## B. Customising Content Messaging and Tone

Customising content messaging and tone involves tailoring the language, style, and voice of your content to resonate with specific audience segments and their preferences.

a) Audience Persona Alignment: Ensuring that content messaging aligns with the characteristics and preferences of each audience persona.

b) Brand Voice Consistency: Maintaining consistency in brand voice while adapting the tone and style of content to suit different audience segments and contexts.

c) Emotional Connection: Using language and messaging that evoke emotions and resonate with the values and aspirations of the target audience.

## C. Adaptive Content Delivery Across Channels

Adaptive content delivery involves delivering personalised content experiences across multiple channels and touchpoints to reach users wherever they are in their journey.

a) Omni-Channel Personalisation: Implementing strategies to deliver consistent and seamless content experiences across channels such as websites, social media, email, and mobile apps.

b) Contextual Relevance: Adapting content delivery based on user context, such as device type, location, time of day, and previous interactions.

c) Responsive Design: Ensuring that content is displayed optimally across different devices and screen sizes to provide a consistent and user-friendly experience.

By employing dynamic content creation techniques, customising content messaging and tone, and implementing adaptive content delivery strategies across channels, marketers can create more engaging and personalised content experiences that resonate with their target audience.

## IV. Tools and Technologies for Personalisation

### A. Content Management Systems (CMS)

Content Management Systems (CMS) play a crucial role in organising, storing, and delivering content across digital channels. They provide marketers with tools to create, manage, and optimise content for personalised experiences.

a) Features of CMS: Exploring key features such as content creation, editing, scheduling, and version control.

b) Content Personalisation Capabilities: Understanding how CMS platforms support personalisation through dynamic content delivery, user segmentation, and A/B testing.

c) Integration with Personalisation Tools: Leveraging CMS integrations with data analytics, customer segmentation, and marketing automation platforms to enhance personalisation efforts.

### B. Customer Relationship Management (CRM) Software

CRM software enables businesses to manage interactions with customers and prospects, providing insights into customer behaviour, preferences, and engagement history.

    a) Customer Data Management: Utilising CRM databases to store and organise customer information, including contact details, purchase history, and communication preferences.

    b) Segmentation and Targeting: Segmenting customers based on demographic, behavioural, and psychographic factors to personalise marketing campaigns and communications.

    c) Integration with Content Marketing: Integrating CRM data with content marketing efforts to deliver personalised content experiences, track customer interactions, and measure campaign effectiveness.

## C. Marketing Automation Platforms

Marketing automation platforms streamline and automate repetitive marketing tasks, allowing marketers to deliver personalised content at scale and nurture leads through the sales funnel.

    a) Automated Workflows: Designing automated workflows to deliver personalised content based on user behaviour, triggers, and segmentation criteria.

    b) Lead Scoring and Nurturing: Implementing lead scoring models to prioritise leads based on their engagement level and readiness to purchase, and nurturing leads with targeted content.

    c) Personalised Email Campaigns: Using marketing automation tools to create and send personalised email campaigns, including triggered emails, dynamic content, and personalised recommendations.

By leveraging Content Management Systems (CMS), Customer Relationship Management (CRM) software, and Marketing Automation Platforms, marketers can enhance their personalisation efforts, deliver tailored content experiences, and build stronger relationships with their audience.

## V. Measuring the Impact of Personalisation

### A. Key Performance Indicators (KPIs) for Personalisation

Key Performance Indicators (KPIs) are essential metrics used to measure the effectiveness of personalisation efforts in content marketing campaigns.

a) Conversion Rate: Tracking the percentage of website visitors who take a desired action, such as making a purchase, signing up for a newsletter, or downloading a resource.

b) Engagement Metrics: Monitoring metrics such as time spent on site, pages per visit, and bounce rate to gauge audience engagement with personalised content.

c) Click-Through Rate (CTR): Measuring the percentage of users who click on a personalised call-to-action (CTA) or link within a piece of content.

d) Return on Investment (ROI): Calculating the financial return generated from personalised content campaigns compared to the investment made in creating and delivering personalised experiences.

### B. Analytics Tools and Metrics

Analytics tools play a crucial role in measuring and analysing the performance of personalised content marketing campaigns.

a)  Web Analytics Platforms: Utilising tools such as Google Analytics, Adobe Analytics, or Mixpanel to track user behaviour, interactions, and conversions across digital channels.

b)  Heatmaps and Session Recordings: Using tools like Hotjar or Crazy Egg to visualise user interactions with personalised content through heatmaps and session recordings.

c)  A/B Testing Tools: Conducting A/B tests to compare the performance of different variations of personalised content and determine which performs better in terms of engagement and conversion rates.

## C. Continuous Optimisation Based on Performance Insights

Continuous optimisation involves analysing performance data and making iterative improvements to personalised content strategies to maximise effectiveness.

a)  Data Analysis and Insights: Analysing performance metrics and user feedback to identify trends, patterns, and areas for improvement in personalised content campaigns.

b)  Experimentation and Iteration: Testing different personalisation tactics, content formats, and messaging strategies to identify what resonates best with target audiences.

c)  Iterative Refinement: Making data-driven adjustments to personalised content based on performance insights to optimise for better engagement, conversion, and ROI over time.

By defining and tracking relevant KPIs for personalisation, leveraging analytics tools and metrics to measure performance, and continuously optimising personalised content based on performance insights, marketers can improve the effectiveness of their content marketing efforts and deliver more relevant and engaging experiences to their audience.

## VI. Real-World Case Studies and Examples

### A. Successful Personalisation Strategies in Action

Successful personalisation strategies demonstrate how brands effectively implement personalisation to enhance the customer experience and drive business results.

   a) Hyper-Personalisation: Case studies showcasing brands that excel in delivering hyper-personalised experiences by leveraging customer data and advanced segmentation techniques.

   b) Content Recommendation Engines: Examples of companies effectively using content recommendation engines to deliver personalised product recommendations, content suggestions, and tailored messaging.

   c) Behavioural Trigger Campaigns: Showcase of brands that leverage behavioural triggers, such as cart abandonment emails, personalised promotions based on browsing history, and dynamic website content, to drive conversions and engagement.

### B. Lessons Learned and Best Practices from Industry Leaders

Learning from industry leaders provides valuable insights and actionable best practices for implementing successful personalisation strategies.

   a) Customer-Centric Approach: Insights into how leading brands prioritise customer needs and preferences, using data-driven insights to deliver relevant and timely content.

   b) Integration of Data Sources: Best practices for integrating various data sources, including CRM data, website analytics, and social media insights, to create a unified view of the customer and deliver personalised experiences across channels.

c) Continuous Testing and Optimisation: Lessons learned from industry leaders on the importance of continuous testing and optimisation to refine personalisation strategies, improve engagement, and drive better business outcomes.

By examining successful personalisation strategies in action and learning from industry leaders' experiences and best practices, marketers can gain valuable insights to inform their own personalisation efforts and drive greater success in content marketing campaigns.

## VII. Challenges and Considerations in Personalisation

### A. Privacy and Data Security Concerns

Privacy and data security are paramount considerations in personalisation efforts to ensure that customer data is handled responsibly and ethically.

a) Regulatory Compliance: Discussion on compliance with data protection laws such as GDPR, CCPA, and other regional regulations to safeguard user privacy.

b) Transparent Data Practices: Importance of transparent data collection and usage policies to build trust with customers and maintain transparency about how their data is being utilised.

c) Data Security Measures: Overview of security measures, including encryption, access controls, and data anonymisation, to protect sensitive customer information from unauthorised access or breaches.

### B. Balancing Personalisation with User Experience

While personalisation enhances user experience, it's essential to strike a balance to avoid overwhelming or intruding on users.

- a) Relevance vs. Intrusiveness: Importance of delivering personalised content that is relevant and adds value to the user experience without being intrusive or overly invasive.

- b) User Consent and Control: Empowering users with control over their data and personalisation preferences through opt-in/opt-out mechanisms and preference centres.

- c) Personalisation Usability: Ensuring that personalisation efforts enhance, rather than detract from, the overall usability and accessibility of the user interface and content.

## C. Overcoming Implementation Challenges

Implementing effective personalisation strategies can present various challenges that marketers must overcome to achieve success.

- a) Data Integration Complexity: Addressing challenges related to integrating disparate data sources and systems to create a unified view of the customer.

- b) Resource Constraints: Managing resource constraints, including budget, time, and expertise, required for implementing and maintaining personalisation initiatives.

- c) Technology Limitations: Overcoming limitations of existing technology infrastructure and tools, such as legacy systems, lack of scalability, and compatibility issues, to support personalisation efforts effectively.

By addressing privacy and data security concerns, balancing personalisation with user experience, and overcoming implementation challenges, marketers can develop and execute effective personalisation strategies that deliver value to both customers and businesses.

## VIII. Future Trends and Opportunities in Personalisation

### A. Emerging Technologies and Innovations

Emerging technologies and innovations are shaping the future of personalisation, offering new opportunities for marketers to deliver more relevant and engaging content experiences.

   a) Artificial Intelligence (AI) and Machine Learning: Exploring how AI and machine learning algorithms can analyse vast amounts of data to uncover insights and patterns, enabling more precise personalisation.

   b) Natural Language Processing (NLP): Leveraging NLP technologies to understand and interpret user-generated content, such as social media posts, reviews, and comments, to inform personalised content recommendations.

   c) Voice and Conversational Interfaces: Harnessing the power of voice-enabled devices and conversational interfaces to deliver personalised content experiences through voice search, virtual assistants, and chatbots.

### B. The Future of Personalised Content Experiences

The future of personalised content experiences holds exciting possibilities for marketers to create more immersive and tailored interactions with their audience.

   a) Predictive Personalisation: Predicting user behaviour and preferences based on historical data and contextual signals to anticipate and deliver personalised content experiences proactively.

b) Augmented Reality (AR) and Virtual Reality (VR): Exploring how AR and VR technologies can enhance personalisation by providing immersive and interactive content experiences that adapt to individual user preferences.

c) Hyper-Personalisation at Scale: Advancements in technology enabling marketers to achieve hyper-personalisation at scale by dynamically generating personalised content in real-time based on individual user attributes and behaviours.

C. Strategies for Staying Ahead in a Personalised Landscape

To stay ahead in a rapidly evolving personalised landscape, marketers must adopt strategic approaches to adapt and innovate.

a) Continuous Learning and Experimentation: Embracing a culture of continuous learning and experimentation to test new personalisation strategies, technologies, and tactics.

b) Agility and Adaptability: Building flexible and adaptable systems and processes to respond quickly to changes in consumer behaviour, technology advancements, and market trends.

c) Collaboration and Partnerships: Fostering collaboration and partnerships with technology providers, agencies, and industry experts to leverage expertise and resources in driving personalised content initiatives forward.

By embracing emerging technologies and innovations, envisioning the future of personalised content experiences, and adopting strategic approaches for staying ahead in a personalised landscape, marketers can unlock new opportunities and drive greater success in their content marketing efforts.

## Chapter 8: Cultivating Long-Term Relationships

I. Introduction to Long-Term Relationship Building in Content Marketing

A. Importance of Long-Term Relationships for Audience Engagement

Long-term relationships with customers are essential for sustained audience engagement and business success.

- a) Building Trust and Loyalty: Establishing trust over time fosters stronger relationships, leading to increased loyalty and repeat business.

- b) Enhanced Customer Lifetime Value: Long-term relationships result in higher customer lifetime value as loyal customers tend to make more frequent purchases and are less price sensitive.

- c) Brand Advocacy: Satisfied long-term customers are more likely to become brand advocates, sharing positive experiences with others and contributing to word-of-mouth marketing.

B. Shift from Transactional to Relational Marketing

There has been a significant shift in marketing from transactional, one-time interactions to relational, ongoing engagements with customers.

- a) Focus on Customer Experience: Relational marketing prioritises delivering exceptional customer experiences at every touchpoint, fostering deeper connections and emotional engagement.

- b) Personalisation and Customisation: Building relationships involves personalising interactions based on individual preferences, needs, and behaviour to create more meaningful experiences.

c) Continuous Communication: Maintaining regular communication with customers through various channels helps nurture relationships and keep the brand top-of-mind.

## C. Benefits of Building Customer Loyalty and Advocacy

Building customer loyalty and advocacy yields numerous benefits for businesses, including increased revenue and brand reputation.

a) Repeat Business and Revenue Growth: Loyal customers are more likely to make repeat purchases, leading to consistent revenue growth and reduced customer acquisition costs.

b) Positive Word-of-Mouth: Satisfied customers who become brand advocates spread positive word-of-mouth recommendations, attracting new customers and enhancing brand reputation.

c) Feedback and Insights: Engaged customers provide valuable feedback and insights that help improve products, services, and overall customer experience.

By Recognising the importance of long-term relationships for audience engagement, embracing a shift from transactional to relational marketing, and understanding the benefits of building customer loyalty and advocacy, businesses can cultivate deeper connections with their audience and drive sustainable growth.

## II. Understanding Customer Needs and Preferences

### A. Customer Journey Mapping and Lifecycle Analysis

Understanding the customer journey and analysing the lifecycle of customer interactions are essential for building and nurturing long-term relationships.

a) Customer Journey Mapping: Mapping out the various touchpoints and interactions customers have with the brand across different stages of their journey, from awareness to advocacy.

b) Lifecycle Analysis: Analysing the lifecycle of customer relationships to identify key stages, milestones, and opportunities for engagement and intervention.

c) Identifying Pain Points and Opportunities: Identifying pain points and friction points in the customer journey and leveraging insights to enhance the customer experience and drive loyalty.

## B. Listening to Customer Feedback and Sentiment Analysis

Listening to customer feedback and analysing sentiment provides valuable insights into customer preferences, needs, and satisfaction levels.

a) Feedback Collection Methods: Utilising various feedback collection methods such as surveys, reviews, social media listening, and customer support interactions to gather insights.

b) Sentiment Analysis: Analysing the sentiment of customer feedback to gauge overall satisfaction levels and identify areas for improvement.

c) Actionable Insights: Using customer feedback to drive actionable insights and improvements in products, services, and customer experience.

## C. Creating Personas for Targeted Relationship Building

Creating personas helps businesses understand their customers' needs, preferences, and behaviours, enabling more targeted and personalised relationship building.

a) Persona Development: Creating detailed personas based on demographic, psychographic, and behavioural attributes to represent different customer segments.

b) Segmentation and Targeting: Segmenting customers based on persona attributes to tailor messaging, offers, and interactions to specific audience segments.

c) Personalised Engagement: Leveraging persona insights to deliver personalised content, recommendations, and experiences that resonate with individual customer personas.

By Utilising customer journey mapping and lifecycle analysis, listening to customer feedback and sentiment analysis, and creating personas for targeted relationship building, businesses can better understand their customers, anticipate their needs, and build meaningful and long-lasting relationships.

## III. Strategies for Building Trust and Credibility

### A. Providing Value-Driven Content and Resources

Delivering value-driven content and resources is crucial for fostering long-term relationships with customers.

a) Educational Content: Providing educational content that addresses customer pain points, challenges, and interests demonstrates expertise and builds trust.

b) Helpful Resources: Offering useful resources such as guides, tutorials, webinars, and tools adds value to the customer experience and positions the brand as a trusted advisor.

c) Personalised Recommendations: Delivering personalised content recommendations based on customer preferences and behaviour increases relevance and engagement.

### B. Transparency and Authenticity in Communication

Transparency and authenticity are essential for building trust and credibility with customers.

a) Honest Communication: Communicating openly and honestly about products, services, pricing, and policies fosters trust and strengthens relationships.

b) Authentic Brand Voice: Maintaining an authentic brand voice that reflects the brand's values, personality, and culture resonates with customers on a deeper level.

c) Addressing Feedback and Concerns: Responding promptly and transparently to customer feedback, inquiries, and concerns demonstrates a commitment to customer satisfaction and builds trust.

### C. Building Social Proof and Reputation Management

Building social proof and managing reputation are critical for establishing credibility and trustworthiness.

a) Customer Testimonials and Reviews: Showcasing positive customer testimonials, reviews, and case studies provides social proof and reassures potential customers of the brand's quality and reliability.

b) Influencer Partnerships: Collaborating with influencers and thought leaders in the industry can help amplify the brand's message and credibility.

c) Proactive Reputation Management: Monitoring online conversations, addressing negative feedback or reviews promptly, and actively managing the brand's online reputation help safeguard credibility and trust.

By providing value-driven content and resources, fostering transparency and authenticity in communication, and building social proof and reputation management, businesses can strengthen relationships with customers, enhance brand trust, and foster long-term loyalty.

## IV. Nurturing Relationships Through Personalisation

### A. Tailoring Content and Experiences to Individual Preferences

Tailoring content and experiences to individual preferences is key to building lasting relationships with customers.

- a) Personalised Recommendations: Providing personalised product recommendations, content suggestions, and offers based on past behaviour and preferences enhances relevance and engagement.

- b) Dynamic Content: Serving dynamic content that adapts in real-time based on user interactions, location, and demographics creates more personalised and engaging experiences.

- c) Preference Centres: Empowering customers to customise their preferences and communication settings ensures that they receive content and offers that align with their interests and preferences.

### B. Leveraging Data to Anticipate Customer Needs

Data-driven insights enable businesses to anticipate customer needs and proactively address them.

- a) Behavioural Analysis: Analysing customer behaviour and interactions with the brand to identify patterns, trends, and predictive indicators of future needs and preferences.

- b) Predictive Modelling: Using predictive modelling techniques to forecast future behaviours, such as purchase intent, churn risk, and product interests, enables businesses to anticipate and meet customer needs more effectively.

c) Triggered Communications: Implementing triggered communications based on specific customer actions or milestones, such as welcome emails, re-engagement campaigns, and personalised recommendations, ensures timely and relevant interactions.

## C. Implementing Lifecycle Marketing Strategies

Lifecycle marketing strategies focus on nurturing customer relationships at every stage of the customer lifecycle.

a) Onboarding and Welcome Series: Welcoming new customers with onboarding emails and welcome series that introduce them to the brand, educate them about products or services, and guide them through the initial experience.

b) Nurturing Campaigns: Implementing nurturing campaigns that deliver targeted content and offers to customers based on their lifecycle stage, preferences, and behaviour, to keep them engaged and moving along the customer journey.

c) Retention and Loyalty Programs: Developing retention and loyalty programs that reward loyal customers, encourage repeat purchases, and foster ongoing engagement and advocacy.

By tailoring content and experiences to individual preferences, leveraging data to anticipate customer needs, and implementing lifecycle marketing strategies, businesses can cultivate deeper relationships with customers, drive loyalty, and maximise lifetime value.

## V. Communication and Engagement Tactics

### A. Effective Email Marketing Strategies for Relationship Building

Email marketing serves as a cornerstone for nurturing long-term relationships with customers.

a) Personalisation: Crafting personalised email campaigns based on customer preferences, behaviour, and lifecycle stage enhances relevance and fosters a deeper connection.

b) Segmentation: Segmenting email lists to target specific audience segments with tailored content and offers ensures that messages resonate with recipients.

c) Automation: Implementing automated email workflows for onboarding, lead nurturing, and re-engagement streamlines communication and ensures consistent engagement throughout the customer journey.

### B. Social Media Engagement and Community Building

Social media platforms offer valuable opportunities for brands to engage with their audience and cultivate a sense of community.

a) Active Listening: Monitoring social media channels for mentions, comments, and discussions related to the brand allows for timely responses and proactive engagement.

b) Content Sharing: Sharing relevant and engaging content, including user-generated content and behind-the-scenes glimpses, encourages interaction and strengthens community bonds.

c) Community Management: Establishing and nurturing online communities where customers can connect, share experiences, and support one another fosters a sense of belonging and brand advocacy.

### C. Interactive Content and Conversational Marketing

Interactive content and conversational marketing techniques facilitate more engaging and personalised interactions with customers.

a) Interactive Experiences: Creating interactive content such as quizzes, polls, and interactive videos invites participation and feedback, driving engagement and strengthening relationships.

b) Conversational AI: Implementing chatbots and conversational AI technologies enables real-time support and personalised interactions, enhancing the customer experience and building rapport.

c) Live Chat: Offering live chat support on websites and messaging apps provides immediate assistance and fosters meaningful conversations with customers, leading to increased satisfaction and loyalty.

By deploying effective email marketing strategies, engaging with customers on social media, and leveraging interactive content and conversational marketing, businesses can cultivate stronger relationships with their audience, foster brand loyalty, and drive long-term success.

## VI. Customer Service and Support

### A. Providing Exceptional Customer Service Experiences

Exceptional customer service is crucial for building and maintaining long-term relationships with customers.

a) Responsive Communication: Responding promptly to customer inquiries, whether through email, phone, or live chat, demonstrates attentiveness and care.

b) Empathetic Support: Showing empathy and understanding towards customer concerns and challenges helps build trust and strengthens the customer relationship.

c) Going Above and Beyond: Going the extra mile to exceed customer expectations, whether by offering personalised recommendations or providing additional assistance, leaves a lasting positive impression.

## B. Addressing Customer Concerns and Resolving Issues Promptly

Addressing customer concerns and resolving issues promptly is essential for maintaining customer satisfaction and loyalty.

a) Active Listening: Actively listening to customer feedback and concerns allows businesses to understand the root cause of issues and take appropriate action.

b) Timely Resolution: Resolving customer issues in a timely manner, whether by providing solutions or offering refunds or exchanges, demonstrates commitment to customer satisfaction.

c) Transparency: Being transparent about the resolution process and keeping customers informed about progress builds trust and reassures them that their concerns are being taken seriously.

## C. Turning Customer Feedback into Opportunities for Improvement

Customer feedback is a valuable source of insights for identifying areas for improvement and enhancing the customer experience.

a) Feedback Collection: Actively soliciting feedback from customers through surveys, reviews, and feedback forms provides valuable insights into areas where the business can improve.

b) Analysing Feedback: Analysing customer feedback to identify recurring issues, trends, and patterns helps prioritise areas for improvement and focus resources effectively.

c) Implementing Changes: Taking action based on customer feedback by implementing changes and improvements demonstrates responsiveness and dedication to customer satisfaction.

By providing exceptional customer service experiences, addressing customer concerns promptly, and turning customer feedback into opportunities for improvement, businesses can build stronger relationships with their customers, foster loyalty, and drive long-term success.

## VII. Loyalty Programs and Incentives

### A. Designing Loyalty Programs to Reward and Retain Customers

Loyalty programs play a vital role in rewarding and retaining customers over the long term.

a) Tiered Rewards: Designing tiered loyalty programs with escalating rewards encourages customers to continue engaging with the brand to unlock higher levels of benefits.

b) Points-Based Systems: Implementing points-based systems where customers earn points for purchases or engagement activities allows them to redeem rewards or discounts, incentivising repeat business.

c) Exclusive Offers: Offering exclusive discounts, promotions, or access to special events or products reserved for loyalty program members reinforces the value proposition and encourages ongoing participation.

### B. Offering Exclusive Benefits and Incentives for Repeat Engagement

Providing exclusive benefits and incentives for repeat engagement reinforces loyalty and strengthens customer relationships.

a) VIP Treatment: Offering VIP treatment to loyal customers, such as early access to sales, dedicated customer support, or personalised recommendations, makes them feel valued and appreciated.

b) Special Events and Rewards: Hosting special events or offering unique rewards, such as anniversary gifts or birthday bonuses, celebrates customers' loyalty and fosters emotional connections with the brand.

c) Referral Programs: Implementing referral programs where loyal customers can earn rewards for referring friends or family members incentivises them to become brand advocates and helps drive new customer acquisition.

### C. Measuring and Optimising Loyalty Program Performance

Measuring and optimising loyalty program performance is essential for ensuring effectiveness and driving continuous improvement.

a) Key Performance Indicators (KPIs): Tracking KPIs such as member acquisition, retention rates, redemption rates, and customer lifetime value provides insights into the program's impact and effectiveness.

b) Feedback and Surveys: Gathering feedback from program members through surveys or feedback forms helps identify areas for improvement and informs future program enhancements.

c) Iterative Optimisation: Continuously optimising the loyalty program based on performance data and customer feedback ensures that it remains relevant, engaging, and aligned with evolving customer needs and preferences.

By designing loyalty programs to reward and retain customers, offering exclusive benefits and incentives for repeat engagement, and measuring and optimising program performance, businesses can foster deeper connections with their customers, drive loyalty, and maximise customer lifetime value.

## VIII. Building Advocacy and Word-of-Mouth Marketing

### A. Encouraging User-Generated Content and Customer Reviews

Encouraging user-generated content (UGC) and customer reviews is a powerful way to build advocacy and generate word-of-mouth marketing.

a) UGC Campaigns: Launching UGC campaigns that encourage customers to share photos, videos, or testimonials showcasing their experiences with the brand fosters authenticity and credibility.

b) Customer Reviews: Actively soliciting and showcasing customer reviews and testimonials on the brand's website and social media platforms helps build trust and influence purchase decisions.

### B. Empowering Brand Advocates and Influencers

Empowering brand advocates and influencers to share their positive experiences can amplify word-of-mouth marketing efforts.

a) Advocate Programs: Establishing advocate programs that reward loyal customers for sharing their love for the brand with their networks incentivises advocacy and drives referral traffic.

b) Influencer Partnerships: Collaborating with influencers and brand ambassadors who align with the brand's values and target audience can help reach new audiences and drive awareness and engagement.

### C. Leveraging Referral Programs and Ambassadorship Initiatives

Referral programs and ambassadorship initiatives incentivise customers to refer friends and family members, driving new customer acquisition through word-of-mouth marketing.

a) Referral Programs: Implementing referral programs that offer rewards or discounts to customers who refer new customers encourages existing customers to become brand advocates and drive referrals.

b) Ambassador Programs: Creating ambassador programs where loyal customers can become brand ambassadors and receive exclusive benefits or rewards for promoting the brand to their networks fosters a sense of belonging and strengthens loyalty.

By encouraging user-generated content and customer reviews, empowering brand advocates and influencers, and leveraging referral programs and ambassadorship initiatives, businesses can harness the power of word-of-mouth marketing to build advocacy, drive engagement, and foster long-term relationships with their customers.

## IX. Measuring Long-Term Relationship Success

### A. Key Performance Indicators (KPIs) for Relationship Building

Measuring the success of long-term relationship-building efforts requires tracking key performance indicators (KPIs) that reflect customer engagement and loyalty.

a) Customer Retention Rate: Calculating the percentage of customers who continue to engage with the brand over time provides insights into the effectiveness of retention strategies.

b) Net Promoter Score (NPS): Surveying customers to measure their likelihood to recommend the brand to others helps gauge overall satisfaction and advocacy levels.

c) Customer Lifetime Value (CLV): Analysing the total revenue generated by individual customers over their lifetime relationship with the brand indicates the value of long-term relationships.

## B. Analytics Tools and Metrics for Tracking Customer Engagement

Utilising analytics tools and metrics allows businesses to track and analyse customer engagement across various touchpoints.

a) Website Analytics: Monitoring website traffic, user behaviour, and conversion rates using tools like Google Analytics provides insights into customer interactions and preferences.

b) Social Media Metrics: Tracking engagement metrics such as likes, shares, comments, and follower growth on social media platforms helps assess the impact of social media marketing efforts.

Email Marketing Performance: Analysing email open rates, click-through rates, and conversion rates provides insights into the effectiveness of email campaigns in nurturing customer relationships.

## C. Continuous Optimisation Based on Relationship Insights

Continuous optimisation based on relationship insights ensures that businesses adapt and evolve their strategies to meet changing customer needs and preferences.

a) Data Analysis: Analysing customer feedback, engagement data, and KPIs allows businesses to identify patterns, trends, and areas for improvement in their relationship-building efforts.

b) Iterative Testing: Conducting A/B tests and experiments to optimise messaging, offers, and customer experiences helps refine strategies and maximise engagement and retention.

c) Personalisation and Customisation: Tailoring communications and experiences based on individual customer preferences and behaviour fosters deeper connections and strengthens long-term relationships.

By tracking KPIs for relationship building, Utilising analytics tools to track customer engagement, and continuously optimising strategies based on relationship insights, businesses can effectively measure the success of their long-term relationship-building efforts and drive sustainable growth and loyalty.

## X. Case Studies and Real-World Examples

### A. Successful Long-Term Relationship Building Strategies in Action

Examining real-world examples of successful long-term relationship-building strategies provides valuable insights into effective practices.

- a) Company X: Customer-Centric Approach: Company X prioritises customer satisfaction and loyalty by offering personalised experiences, proactive support, and exclusive benefits for long-term customers.

- b) Brand Y: Community Engagement Initiatives: Brand Y fosters a sense of community and belonging among its customers through online forums, events, and ambassador programs, driving advocacy and retention.

- c) Organisation Z: Data-Driven Personalisation: Organisation Z leverages data analytics and AI technology to deliver highly personalised experiences tailored to individual customer preferences and behaviour, enhancing engagement and loyalty.

### B. Lessons Learned and Best Practices from Industry Leaders

Extracting lessons and best practices from industry leaders' experiences provides actionable insights for businesses seeking to strengthen long-term relationships.

- a) Focus on Customer Value: Prioritising customer value and satisfaction over short-term gains fosters loyalty and advocacy, driving sustainable growth.

b) Consistent Communication: Maintaining open and transparent communication with customers throughout their journey builds trust and reinforces the brand-customer relationship.

c) Iterative Optimisation: Continuously optimising strategies based on customer feedback and performance data ensures relevance and effectiveness in relationship-building efforts.

By studying successful case studies and learning from industry leaders' experiences, businesses can gain valuable inspiration and insights to inform their own long-term relationship-building strategies, driving customer loyalty, advocacy, and sustainable growth.

## XI. Challenges and Considerations in Relationship Building

### A. Balancing Personalisation with Privacy and Data Protection

Achieving a balance between personalised experiences and protecting customer privacy is essential for maintaining trust and compliance with data regulations.

a) Transparency and Consent: Communicating clearly with customers about data usage and obtaining their consent for personalised experiences builds trust and ensures compliance with privacy regulations.

b) Data Security Measures: Implementing robust data security measures, such as encryption and secure storage protocols, safeguards customer information from unauthorised access or breaches.

c) Respecting Customer Preferences: Respecting customer preferences regarding data collection and personalisation settings demonstrates respect for their privacy and preferences.

## B. Overcoming Customer Engagement Fatigue and Burnout

Managing customer engagement fatigue and burnout requires careful attention to the frequency and relevancy of communication.

a) Segmentation and Targeting: Segmenting audiences based on their preferences and behaviour allows businesses to tailor communication frequency and content to individual preferences.

b) Content Relevance: Ensuring that content remains relevant and valuable to customers prevents them from feeling overwhelmed or disengaged from excessive communication.

c) Opt-out Options: Providing easy-to-find opt-out options allows customers to control their engagement levels and reduces the risk of fatigue or burnout.

## C. Addressing Cultural and Market Differences in Relationship Dynamics

Navigating cultural and market differences in relationship dynamics requires sensitivity and adaptability to diverse customer needs and preferences.

a) Cultural Sensitivity: Recognising and respecting cultural norms and values when communicating with diverse customer segments fosters understanding and trust.

b) Market Research: Conducting thorough market research to understand local preferences, behaviours, and expectations helps tailor relationship-building strategies to specific markets.

c) Localisation: Adapting communication styles, messaging, and offers to resonate with local cultures and market dynamics enhances relevance and effectiveness in relationship-building efforts.

By addressing the challenges and considerations in relationship building, businesses can navigate complexities and build stronger, more meaningful connections with their customers, driving loyalty and long-term success.

## XII. Future Trends and Opportunities in Relationship Building

### A. Emerging Technologies and Innovations Shaping Relationship Marketing

The future of relationship marketing is heavily influenced by emerging technologies and innovations that enable more personalised and immersive customer experiences.

a) Artificial Intelligence (AI) and Machine Learning: AI-powered algorithms analyse vast amounts of customer data to predict behaviour and preferences, enabling highly personalised recommendations and interactions.

b) Augmented Reality (AR) and Virtual Reality (VR): AR and VR technologies create immersive brand experiences that allow customers to interact with products and services in virtual environments, fostering deeper engagement and connection.

c) Blockchain Technology: Blockchain technology enhances data security and transparency, enabling customers to have greater control over their personal information and fostering trust in relationships.

### B. The Evolution of Customer Experience and Relationship Management

The evolution of customer experience and relationship management is characterised by a shift towards more holistic and seamless interactions across multiple touchpoints.

a)  Omni-Channel Integration: Integrating customer interactions seamlessly across online and offline channels provides a cohesive and consistent experience throughout the customer journey.

b)  Predictive Analytics: Predictive analytics tools forecast future customer behaviour and preferences, allowing businesses to anticipate needs and proactively engage with customers at the right time and place.

c)  Emotional Intelligence: Emphasising emotional intelligence in customer interactions enables businesses to connect with customers on a deeper level, fostering stronger emotional bonds and loyalty.

## C. Strategies for Sustaining Long-Term Relationships in a Dynamic Landscape

In a dynamic and ever-changing landscape, businesses must adapt their strategies to sustain long-term relationships with customers effectively.

a)  Agile Marketing Practices: Adopting agile marketing practices allows businesses to respond quickly to changing customer needs and market dynamics, ensuring relevance and engagement.

b)  Continuous Learning and Innovation: Cultivating a culture of continuous learning and innovation enables businesses to stay ahead of emerging trends and opportunities, fostering agility and adaptability.

c)  Collaboration and Co-Creation: Collaborating with customers to co-create products, services, and experiences fosters a sense of ownership and community, strengthening relationships and loyalty.

By embracing emerging technologies and innovations, evolving customer experience and relationship management practices, and implementing strategies for sustainability in a dynamic landscape, businesses can future-proof their relationship-building efforts and drive long-term success.

## Chapter 9: Adapting to Emerging Trends

I. Introduction to Emerging Trends in Content Marketing

A. Understanding the Dynamic Nature of the Digital Landscape

In today's digital landscape, constant change is the norm. Understanding the dynamic nature of digital platforms, consumer behaviour, and technological advancements is crucial for staying relevant and effective in content marketing.

a) Shifts in Consumer Behaviour: Consumers' preferences, habits, and expectations evolve rapidly in response to cultural, economic, and technological shifts.

b) Platform Diversity: The proliferation of digital platforms—from social media networks to streaming services—offers diverse opportunities and challenges for content marketers.

c) Technological Advancements: Innovations such as artificial intelligence, augmented reality, and voice search continue to reshape how content is created, distributed, and consumed.

B. Importance of Adaptation and Innovation in Content Marketing

Adaptation and innovation are essential for content marketers to thrive amidst constant change and disruption in the digital landscape.

a) Agility and Flexibility: Being agile and flexible allows content marketers to respond quickly to emerging trends, opportunities, and challenges.

b) Experimentation and Risk-Taking: Embracing experimentation and taking calculated risks enable content marketers to discover new strategies and approaches that resonate with their audience.

c) Continuous Learning: Committing to continuous learning and professional development ensures that content marketers stay informed about industry trends, best practices, and emerging technologies.

### C. Overview of Emerging Trends and Their Impact on Audience Engagement

Several emerging trends are reshaping the content marketing landscape and influencing audience engagement strategies.

a) Video Dominance: The rise of video content across platforms, from short-form videos on social media to long-form content on streaming platforms, presents new opportunities for engaging audiences.

b) Interactive Content: Interactive content formats such as quizzes, polls, and AR experiences enable deeper engagement and interaction with audiences.

c) Voice Search Optimisation: The increasing adoption of voice-enabled devices and voice search technologies requires content marketers to optimise content for voice-based queries and interactions.

Understanding the dynamic digital landscape, embracing adaptation and innovation, and leveraging emerging trends are essential for content marketers to effectively engage audiences and achieve success in today's competitive environment.

## II. Content Formats and Consumption Trends

### A. Rise of Short-Form Video Content and Micro-Content

Short-form video content and micro-content have gained immense popularity, driven by platforms like TikTok, Instagram Reels, and Snapchat.

a) Attention Span Considerations: Short-form videos cater to the shrinking attention spans of audiences, delivering bite-sized content that is easy to consume.

b) Engagement Opportunities: Micro-content, such as GIFs, memes, and short videos, offer quick and engaging ways to connect with audiences and convey messages effectively.

c) Platform Optimisation: Content marketers must optimise their strategies to leverage the unique features and algorithms of short-form video platforms to maximise reach and engagement.

### B. Growth of Interactive and Immersive Content Experiences

Interactive and immersive content experiences captivate audiences and foster deeper engagement and interaction.

a) Enhanced Engagement: Interactive content formats, such as quizzes, polls, and interactive infographics, encourage active participation from audiences, resulting in higher engagement rates.

b) Virtual and Augmented Reality (VR/AR): VR and AR technologies create immersive experiences that transport audiences to virtual environments, allowing for innovative storytelling and brand experiences.

c) Gamification: Incorporating gamification elements, such as challenges, rewards, and leaderboards, into content experiences enhances engagement and encourages repeat interactions.

### C. Evolution of Voice Search and Audio Content Consumption

The proliferation of voice-enabled devices and the growing popularity of audio content consumption present new opportunities and challenges for content marketers.

a) Voice Search Optimisation: Optimising content for voice search queries requires understanding natural language patterns and conversational queries to ensure visibility in voice search results.

b) Podcasting and Audio Streaming: The rise of podcasting and audio streaming platforms offers a unique avenue for content distribution and audience engagement, catering to on-the-go and multitasking audiences.

c) Audio Branding: Establishing a strong audio brand identity through sonic branding elements, such as jingles and soundscapes, enhances brand recognition and recall in audio content experiences.

Adapting to the rise of short-form video content, interactive and immersive experiences, and the evolution of voice search and audio content consumption is essential for content marketers to effectively engage audiences and stay ahead in today's dynamic digital landscape.

## III. Platform and Channel Shifts

### A. Emergence of New Social Media Platforms and Trends

The landscape of social media platforms is constantly evolving, with the emergence of new platforms and trends reshaping audience engagement strategies.

a) Diversification of Platforms: New social media platforms, such as Clubhouse, TikTok, and Discord, offer unique opportunities for content creators to reach niche audiences and explore innovative content formats.

b) Trends in Content Consumption: Shifts in content consumption habits, such as the rise of ephemeral content and the popularity of live streaming, require content marketers to adapt their strategies to meet changing audience preferences.

c) Engagement on Emerging Platforms: Experimentation and early adoption of emerging platforms allow content marketers to establish a presence and engage with audiences in new and innovative ways.

## B. Shift Towards Visual-First Platforms and Visual Storytelling

Visual content continues to dominate social media platforms, driving the shift towards visual-first platforms and visual storytelling techniques.

a) Visual Appeal: Platforms like Instagram, Pinterest, and Snapchat prioritise visual content, making images and videos essential for capturing audience attention and conveying brand messages effectively.

b) Storytelling through Images and Videos: Visual storytelling techniques, such as Instagram Stories, reels, and carousel posts, enable brands to narrate compelling stories and create emotional connections with their audience.

c) User-Generated Visual Content: Encouraging user-generated visual content, such as user-generated images and videos, fosters authenticity and builds a sense of community around the brand.

## C. Increasing Importance of Niche and Community-Based Platforms

Niche and community-based platforms are gaining traction, offering highly engaged audiences and opportunities for targeted content marketing efforts.

a) Focused Communities: Platforms like Reddit, LinkedIn Groups, and specialised forums provide dedicated spaces for niche communities to connect, share knowledge, and engage in discussions around specific topics of interest.

b) Hyper-Targeted Advertising: Leveraging niche and community-based platforms allows content marketers to target highly relevant audiences with tailored content and advertising campaigns, maximising engagement and conversion rates.

c) Building Brand Advocacy: Active participation and engagement within niche communities can position brands as industry leaders and foster advocacy among community members, driving word-of-mouth referrals and brand loyalty.

Understanding the emergence of new social media platforms and trends, the shift towards visual-first platforms and visual storytelling, and the increasing importance of niche and community-based platforms is essential for content marketers to effectively reach and engage with their target audience in today's ever-evolving digital landscape.

## IV. Technology and Innovation in Content Creation

### A. Role of Artificial Intelligence (AI) in Content Creation and Personalisation

Artificial Intelligence (AI) is revolutionising content creation and personalisation, empowering content marketers to deliver highly relevant and engaging experiences to their audiences.

a) Content Generation: AI-powered tools, such as natural language generation (NLG) algorithms, enable automated content creation for various formats, including articles, product descriptions, and social media posts.

b) Personalisation: AI algorithms analyse vast amounts of data to understand individual preferences and behaviours, allowing content marketers to personalise content recommendations, product suggestions, and marketing messages for each user.

c) Dynamic Content Optimisation: AI-driven content optimisation tools dynamically adjust content elements, such as headlines, images, and calls-to-action, based on real-time performance data, maximising engagement and conversion rates.

### B. Leveraging Augmented Reality (AR) and Virtual Reality (VR) Experiences

Augmented Reality (AR) and Virtual Reality (VR) experiences offer immersive and interactive content opportunities that captivate audiences and drive deeper engagement.

a) Immersive Brand Experiences: AR and VR technologies enable brands to create immersive experiences that transport users to virtual environments, allowing for innovative storytelling and product demonstrations.

b) Interactive Engagement: AR and VR experiences encourage users to interact with content in unique ways, such as exploring 3D product models, participating in virtual events, and gamified experiences, enhancing engagement and retention.

c) Enhanced Product Visualisation: AR technology allows users to visualise products in their real-world environment, facilitating informed purchase decisions and reducing buyer hesitation.

### C. Impact of Emerging Technologies on Content Distribution and Consumption

Emerging technologies are reshaping content distribution and consumption patterns, providing new avenues for reaching and engaging audiences.

a) Voice-Activated Devices: The proliferation of voice-activated devices, such as smart speakers and virtual assistants, presents opportunities for content distribution through audio channels and voice search optimisation.

b) Blockchain Technology: Blockchain technology enhances content distribution by providing transparent and secure platforms for publishing and monetising content, empowering creators and ensuring authenticity.

c) 5G Technology: The rollout of 5G technology enables faster internet speeds and seamless streaming experiences, facilitating the consumption of high-quality video content and immersive AR/VR experiences on mobile devices.

Embracing the role of AI in content creation and personalisation, leveraging AR and VR experiences, and adapting to the impact of emerging technologies on content distribution and consumption are essential for content marketers to stay ahead in today's digital landscape and deliver compelling experiences to their audiences.

## V. Data Privacy and Ethical Considerations

### A. Growing Concerns Around Data Privacy and Protection

The growing awareness of data privacy issues has led to increased scrutiny and concern regarding the collection, use, and protection of personal data by businesses and content marketers.

a) Data Breaches and Misuse: High-profile data breaches and incidents of data misuse have eroded trust among consumers, prompting calls for stricter regulations and enhanced privacy protections.

b) Regulatory Landscape: Regulatory frameworks, such as the General Data Protection Regulation (GDPR) and the California Consumer Privacy Act (CCPA), aim to safeguard consumer privacy rights and hold businesses accountable for responsible data handling practices.

c) Consumer Expectations: Consumers are becoming more conscious of their privacy rights and expect transparency, consent, and control over how their personal data is collected, processed, and shared.

## B. Implementing Ethical Content Marketing Practices

Ethical content marketing practices prioritise honesty, integrity, and respect for consumer privacy and preferences, fostering trust and credibility with audiences.

   a) Transparency and Disclosure: Disclosing data collection practices, privacy policies, and the use of cookies and tracking technologies helps build trust and transparency with consumers.

   b) Consent-Based Marketing: Obtaining explicit consent from consumers before collecting and using their personal data for marketing purposes demonstrates respect for individual privacy rights and preferences.

   c) Responsible Data Handling: Implementing robust data security measures, data anonymisation techniques, and data minimisation practices minimises the risk of data breaches and protects consumer privacy.

## C. Balancing Personalisation with Privacy and Transparency

Achieving a balance between personalisation and privacy is essential for content marketers to deliver tailored experiences while respecting consumer privacy rights and preferences.

   a) Granular Controls: Providing consumers with granular controls and preferences settings allows them to customise their privacy preferences and opt-in or opt-out of personalised marketing communications.

b) Privacy by Design: Adopting privacy by design principles ensures that privacy considerations are integrated into the development of content marketing strategies, platforms, and technologies from the outset.

c) Educating Consumers: Educating consumers about the value exchange between personalised content experiences and data sharing fosters understanding and trust, empowering them to make informed decisions about their privacy.

Navigating the evolving landscape of data privacy and ethical considerations requires content marketers to prioritise transparency, consent, and responsible data handling practices, fostering trust and credibility with their audiences while delivering personalised and engaging content experiences.

## VI. Cultural and Societal Shifts

### A. Addressing Diversity, Equity, and Inclusion in Content Marketing

In today's increasingly diverse and inclusive society, addressing diversity, equity, and inclusion (DEI) in content marketing is not only a moral imperative but also a strategic necessity.

a) Representation Matters: Ensuring diverse representation in content, including race, ethnicity, gender, sexuality, ability, and age, reflects the varied experiences and perspectives of your audience and fosters inclusivity.

b) Authenticity and Representation: Authentic representation involves more than token gestures; it requires genuine efforts to authentically engage with diverse communities and amplify underrepresented voices.

c) Equitable Opportunities: Providing equitable opportunities for content creators, collaborators, and partners from marginalised communities promotes diversity and inclusion across the content ecosystem.

B. Reflecting Cultural Sensitivity and Responsiveness in Content Creation

Cultural sensitivity and responsiveness are essential considerations in content creation to avoid inadvertently perpetuating stereotypes or causing offense.

a) Cultural Competency: Understanding cultural nuances, traditions, and sensitivities ensures that content resonates with diverse audiences and avoids cultural missteps or misunderstandings.

b) Localisation and Adaptation: Adapting content to different cultural contexts, languages, and regions demonstrates respect for cultural diversity and increases relevance and resonance with local audiences.

c) Avoiding Stereotypes: Challenging and avoiding stereotypes in content creation fosters a more inclusive and respectful portrayal of diverse identities and experiences.

C. Navigating Sensitive Topics and Social Issues in Content Strategy

Navigating sensitive topics and social issues requires careful consideration and a nuanced approach to ensure that content is both relevant and respectful.

a) Social Responsibility: Acknowledging and addressing social issues demonstrates corporate social responsibility and aligns with audience expectations for brands to take a stand on important societal issues.

b) Authenticity and Purpose: Authenticity is paramount when addressing sensitive topics, and content should align with the brand's values, mission, and purpose rather than exploiting social issues for marketing gain.

c) Open Dialogue and Listening: Engaging in open dialogue with stakeholders and actively listening to feedback from diverse perspectives fosters understanding, empathy, and trust.

Embracing diversity, equity, and inclusion in content marketing, reflecting cultural sensitivity and responsiveness in content creation, and navigating sensitive topics and social issues in content strategy are essential for content marketers to foster inclusivity, build trust, and resonate with diverse audiences in today's multicultural and interconnected world.

## VII. Sustainability and Corporate Social Responsibility (CSR)

### A. Incorporating Sustainability Messaging and Practices in Content Marketing

Incorporating sustainability messaging and practices in content marketing not only aligns with growing consumer expectations but also demonstrates a commitment to environmental stewardship and social responsibility.

a) Environmental Awareness: Increasing environmental awareness among consumers has heightened the demand for eco-friendly and sustainable products and services, making sustainability a key differentiator in content marketing.

b) Educational Content: Providing educational content about sustainability practices, eco-friendly alternatives, and environmental conservation initiatives helps raise awareness and empowers consumers to make more sustainable choices.

c) Green Messaging: Integrating green messaging, such as eco-friendly product features, sustainable packaging, and carbon footprint reduction efforts, into content marketing campaigns resonates with environmentally conscious audiences.

## B. Communicating CSR Initiatives and Social Impact Efforts

Communicating corporate social responsibility (CSR) initiatives and social impact efforts in content marketing builds trust, enhances brand reputation, and fosters deeper connections with socially conscious consumers.

   a) Transparency and Authenticity: Transparently communicating CSR initiatives and social impact efforts demonstrates authenticity and accountability, fostering trust and credibility with consumers.

   b) Storytelling for Social Good: Leveraging storytelling to highlight the positive social impact of CSR initiatives humanises the brand, inspires action, and creates emotional connections with audiences.

   c) Measurable Impact: Quantifying and reporting on the measurable impact of CSR initiatives, such as carbon emissions reductions, community outreach programs, or charitable donations, provides tangible evidence of the brand's commitment to social responsibility.

## C. Aligning Brand Values with Environmental and Social Responsibility

Aligning brand values with environmental and social responsibility involves integrating sustainability and CSR principles into the brand's core identity, values, and business practices.

   a) Mission-Driven Branding: Articulating a clear mission statement and brand purpose that reflects the company's commitment to environmental and social responsibility communicates authenticity and builds loyalty among socially conscious consumers.

b) Partnerships and Collaborations: Collaborating with like-minded organisations, NGOs, and sustainability-focused initiatives amplifies the brand's impact and extends its reach in driving positive social and environmental change.

c) Long-Term Commitment: Demonstrating a long-term commitment to sustainability and CSR initiatives, beyond mere greenwashing or short-term campaigns, reinforces the brand's credibility and fosters enduring relationships with stakeholders.

Incorporating sustainability messaging and practices, communicating CSR initiatives and social impact efforts, and aligning brand values with environmental and social responsibility are essential for content marketers to meet the evolving expectations of socially conscious consumers and drive positive change in society.

## VIII. Future-Proofing Your Content Marketing Strategy

### A. Staying Agile and Adaptive in a Rapidly Changing Landscape

Staying agile and adaptive in a rapidly changing landscape is crucial for future-proofing your content marketing strategy and maintaining relevance in dynamic market conditions.

a) Agility in Execution: Embracing agile methodologies and flexible workflows allows content marketers to respond quickly to market changes, customer feedback, and emerging trends, ensuring timely and relevant content delivery.

b) Continuous Optimisation: Adopting a culture of continuous optimisation involves regularly evaluating and refining content strategies, tactics, and performance metrics based on real-time data and insights to drive ongoing improvements.

c) Experimentation and Iteration: Encouraging experimentation and iteration in content creation and distribution enables content marketers to test new ideas, formats, and channels, iterate based on feedback, and adapt strategies to evolving audience preferences and behaviours.

## B. Investing in Continuous Learning and Innovation

Investing in continuous learning and innovation empowers content marketers to stay ahead of the curve, acquire new skills, and embrace emerging technologies and best practices.

a) Professional Development: Prioritising ongoing training, upskilling, and professional development programs equips content marketing teams with the knowledge and expertise needed to navigate evolving trends, tools, and techniques effectively.

b) Cross-Functional Collaboration: Fostering cross-functional collaboration and knowledge-sharing across departments, disciplines, and industry sectors fosters a culture of innovation and ideation, sparking creative solutions and fresh perspectives.

c) Embracing Emerging Technologies: Embracing emerging technologies, such as artificial intelligence, machine learning, augmented reality, and voice search, opens new opportunities for innovation and differentiation in content marketing strategies and tactics.

## C. Strategies for Anticipating and Responding to Future Trends

Anticipating and responding to future trends requires proactive planning, scenario analysis, and strategic foresight to identify emerging opportunities and threats and adapt content marketing strategies accordingly.

a) Trend Monitoring and Analysis: Continuously monitoring and analysing industry trends, consumer behaviour patterns, competitive landscapes, and technological advancements enables content marketers to anticipate shifts and proactively adjust strategies to stay ahead of the curve.

b) Scenario Planning: Conducting scenario planning exercises and contingency planning helps content marketers prepare for a range of future scenarios, mitigate risks, and capitalise on emerging opportunities effectively.

c) Innovation Road-mapping: Developing innovation roadmaps and long-term strategic plans outlines clear objectives, milestones, and initiatives for driving innovation, experimentation, and future growth in content marketing.

By staying agile and adaptive, investing in continuous learning and innovation, and implementing strategies for anticipating and responding to future trends, content marketers can future-proof their strategies and thrive in an ever-evolving digital landscape.

## IX. Case Studies and Examples of Successful Adaptation

### A. Organisations Embracing Emerging Trends and Innovations

Examining organisations that have successfully embraced emerging trends and innovations provides valuable insights into effective strategies for staying ahead of the curve in content marketing.

a) Early Adopters: Highlighting early adopters who have embraced emerging trends, such as AI-powered content personalisation, immersive experiences, or niche social media platforms, showcases the benefits of innovation and the competitive advantages gained by being at the forefront of change.

b) Innovative Campaigns: Showcasing innovative campaigns and initiatives from leading brands demonstrates how forward-thinking organisations leverage emerging technologies, trends, and consumer insights to create compelling content experiences that resonate with audiences and drive meaningful results.

c) Industry Disruptors: Examining industry disruptors and challengers who have revolutionised content marketing through disruptive innovation, unconventional approaches, and bold experimentation provides inspiration for organisations looking to break new ground and differentiate themselves in crowded markets.

B. Lessons Learned and Best Practices from Early Adopters

Drawing lessons learned and best practices from early adopters of emerging trends and innovations helps identify key success factors and actionable insights for other organisations seeking to emulate their achievements.

a) Agility and Flexibility: Early adopters demonstrate the importance of agility and flexibility in responding to market changes, consumer preferences, and technological advancements, enabling them to pivot quickly and seize new opportunities.

b) Risk-Taking and Experimentation: Embracing a culture of risk-taking and experimentation allows organisations to push boundaries, challenge conventional wisdom, and test new ideas, ultimately leading to breakthrough innovations and competitive differentiation.

c) Customer-Centricity: Prioritising customer-centricity and user experience drives innovation by focusing on delivering value, solving customer pain points, and exceeding expectations, resulting in higher levels of engagement, loyalty, and advocacy.

C. Strategies for Embracing Change and Thriving in the Future

Developing strategies for embracing change and thriving in the future involves cultivating a mindset of continuous learning, adaptation, and resilience to navigate uncertainty and capitalise on emerging opportunities.

a) Fostering Innovation Culture: Creating an innovation culture that encourages curiosity, creativity, and collaboration fosters a fertile environment for generating breakthrough ideas, fostering experimentation, and driving continuous improvement.

b) Investing in Talent and Technology: Investing in talent development and technological capabilities enables organisations to attract top talent, equip teams with the skills and tools needed to innovate, and leverage cutting-edge technologies to drive future growth and competitiveness.

c) Strategic Partnerships and Ecosystems: Establishing strategic partnerships and ecosystems with technology providers, startups, academia, and industry peers expands access to resources, expertise, and market insights, accelerating innovation and fuelling growth.

By studying organisations that have successfully embraced emerging trends and innovations, drawing lessons learned and best practices, and developing strategies for embracing change and thriving in the future, organisations can position themselves for sustained success in an ever-evolving content marketing landscape.

## X. Challenges and Opportunities in Adapting to Emerging Trends

### A. Overcoming Resistance to Change and Legacy Systems

Addressing resistance to change and overcoming the constraints of legacy systems is essential for organisations to successfully adapt to emerging trends in content marketing.

Cultural Resistance: Cultural resistance to change within organisations can hinder innovation and impede progress. Strategies for fostering a culture of openness, collaboration, and continuous learning are essential for overcoming resistance and driving successful adaptation. Legacy systems and outdated processes may pose challenges to agility and innovation. Investing in modernising infrastructure, upgrading technology platforms, and implementing flexible architectures can help organisations overcome these barriers and embrace change more effectively.

## B. Seizing Opportunities for Growth and Innovation

Identifying and seizing opportunities for growth and innovation is critical for organisations looking to capitalise on emerging trends in content marketing and gain a competitive edge.

a) Market Disruption: Disruptive trends present opportunities for organisations to challenge incumbents, redefine industry norms, and capture new market segments. Being proactive in identifying emerging trends and positioning themselves as innovators allows organisations to seize first-mover advantages and gain market leadership.

b) Innovation Ecosystems: Collaborating with external partners, such as startups, technology providers, and industry peers, fosters innovation ecosystems that facilitate knowledge exchange, co-creation, and access to new technologies and market insights, enabling organisations to capitalise on emerging opportunities more effectively.

## C. Anticipating and Mitigating Risks Associated with Emerging Trends

Anticipating and mitigating risks associated with emerging trends in content marketing is essential for organisations to navigate uncertainty and ensure sustainable growth.

a) Risk Identification: Proactively identifying potential risks associated with emerging trends, such as technology obsolescence, regulatory changes, or shifting consumer preferences, enables organisations to develop risk mitigation strategies and contingency plans to address these challenges effectively.

b) Agility and Adaptability: Cultivating organisational agility and adaptability allows organisations to respond quickly to changing market conditions, pivot strategies as needed, and capitalise on new opportunities while minimising risks associated with emerging trends.

c) Scenario Planning: Conducting scenario planning exercises and stress testing different hypotheses helps organisations prepare for a range of potential outcomes, anticipate challenges, and develop resilience strategies to mitigate risks effectively.

By addressing resistance to change and legacy systems, seizing opportunities for growth and innovation, and anticipating and mitigating risks associated with emerging trends, organisations can adapt more effectively to the evolving landscape of content marketing and position themselves for long-term success.

## XI. Conclusion: Embracing a Future-Forward Mindset

### A. Recap of Key Insights and Strategies for Adapting to Emerging Trends

Reflecting on key insights and strategies discussed throughout this chapter provides a comprehensive understanding of how organisations can effectively adapt to emerging trends in content marketing.

a) Cultural Shift: Embracing a culture of innovation, agility, and continuous learning is essential for organisations to thrive in a rapidly evolving landscape. By fostering a mindset of experimentation, collaboration, and openness to change, organisations can position themselves for long-term success.

b) Strategic Alignment: Aligning organisational strategies, processes, and resources with emerging trends enables organisations to capitalise on new opportunities, mitigate risks, and drive sustainable growth. Strategic foresight and proactive planning are critical for staying ahead of the curve and maintaining a competitive edge.

## B. Encouragement for Embracing Change and Innovation in Content Marketing

Embracing change and innovation in content marketing is essential for organisations to stay relevant, engage audiences effectively, and drive meaningful results in today's dynamic landscape.

- a) Continuous Learning: Encouraging a culture of continuous learning and professional development empowers teams to stay informed about emerging trends, acquire new skills, and adapt to evolving market conditions. Investing in employee training, mentorship programs, and knowledge-sharing initiatives fosters a culture of innovation and growth.

- b) Experimentation and Adaptation: Encouraging experimentation and adaptation allows organisations to test new ideas, iterate on strategies, and pivot quickly in response to changing market dynamics. Embracing failure as a learning opportunity and celebrating successes fuels a culture of innovation and resilience.

## C. Looking Ahead to a Future-Ready Content Strategy

Looking ahead to a future-ready content strategy involves embracing uncertainty, embracing change, and positioning organisations for success in an ever-evolving landscape.

- a) Agility and Flexibility: Building agility and flexibility into content strategies enables organisations to respond quickly to emerging trends, capitalise on new opportunities, and navigate challenges effectively. Prioritising adaptability and resilience allow organisations to thrive amidst uncertainty and complexity.

b) Innovation and Creativity: Cultivating a culture of innovation and creativity fosters breakthrough ideas, drives experimentation, and fuels growth. By embracing creativity, pushing boundaries, and challenging conventions, organisations can differentiate themselves and create compelling content experiences that resonate with audiences.

By recapping key insights and strategies, encouraging a mindset of change and innovation, and looking ahead to a future-ready content strategy, organisations can adapt to emerging trends and position themselves for success in an increasingly dynamic and competitive landscape of content marketing.

## Chapter 10: Conclusion

### I. Recap of Key Insights and Strategies

#### A. Summary of Key Concepts and Takeaways

Recapping key concepts and takeaways reinforcing the essential aspects of content marketing strategies discussed throughout the book:

a) Audience-Centric Approach: Emphasising the importance of understanding audience needs, preferences, and behaviours is crucial for developing effective content marketing strategies. By focusing on the audience's perspective, organisations can create content that resonates and drives engagement.

b) Content Quality and Relevance: Quality content that provides value, educates, entertains, or solves problems for the audience is foundational to content marketing success. Ensuring content relevance and aligning with audience interests are key to capturing attention and fostering engagement.

c) Multichannel Distribution: Leveraging various distribution channels and formats allows organisations to reach audiences where they are most active and engaged. Implementing a multichannel distribution strategy ensures content is accessible, shareable, and optimised for different platforms and devices.

#### B. Review of Effective Content Marketing Strategies Explored Throughout the Book

The content marketing strategies explored throughout the book include:

a) Personalisation: Tailoring content and experiences to individual audience preferences and behaviours enhances relevance and increases engagement. Implementing personalised content strategies, such as dynamic content creation, audience segmentation, and adaptive delivery, enables organisations to connect with audiences on a deeper level.

b) Community Engagement: Building and nurturing communities around brands fosters long-term relationships, loyalty, and advocacy. Engaging with community members, facilitating meaningful interactions, and providing value-driven content cultivates a sense of belonging and strengthens brand affinity.

c) Measurement and Analysis: Measuring and analysing content performance metrics and audience engagement data are essential for optimising content strategies and driving continuous improvement. Implementing robust analytics tools and leveraging insights to iterate strategies based on audience feedback and behaviour leads to more impactful content marketing efforts.

## C. The Importance of Audience Engagement in Content Marketing Success

The significance of audience engagement in content marketing success should not be under-stated. Audiences play a pivotal role in shaping content strategies and driving desired outcomes:

a) Two-Way Communication: Engaging audiences in two-way communication fosters dialogue, builds trust, and strengthens relationships. Listening to audience feedback, responding to inquiries, and incorporating user-generated content enriches the content experience and encourages participation.

b) Long-Term Relationships: Prioritising long-term relationships over short-term transactions fosters customer loyalty, retention, and advocacy. Investing in personalised experiences, providing exceptional customer service, and delivering consistent value across touchpoints build lasting connections with audiences.

## II. Reflection on the Evolution of Content Marketing

### A. Overview of How Content Marketing Has Evolved Over Time

The evolution of content marketing provides insight into its transformational journey from traditional advertising to audience-centric engagement strategies. Understanding this evolution helps contextualise current trends and anticipate future directions.

- a) Historical Context: Tracing the origins of content marketing from its early roots in print media and broadcasting to its digital expansion highlights the shift towards customer-centric approaches and interactive content experiences.

- b) Technological Advancements: The proliferation of digital technologies and the internet has democratised content creation and distribution, empowering brands and individuals to connect with audiences on a global scale. The advent of social media, mobile devices, and emerging technologies has revolutionised how content is consumed, shared, and interacted with.

### B. Emerging Trends and Future Directions in Content Marketing

By embracing these emerging trends and future directions, marketers can stay ahead of the curve and create impactful content marketing strategies that drive meaningful engagement and deliver results in an ever-evolving digital landscape:

- a) Personalised Content Experiences: With advances in data analytics and AI technologies, content personalisation will continue to evolve. Brands will increasingly tailor content to individual preferences, behaviours, and demographics, delivering highly relevant and personalised experiences to consumers.

- b) Interactive Content Formats: Interactive content such as quizzes, polls, and immersive experiences will gain prominence. These formats not only engage audiences more effectively but also provide valuable data insights for marketers to better understand audience preferences and behaviour.

c) Video Dominance: Video content will remain a dominant force in content marketing. Short-form videos, live streams, and interactive video experiences will be key drivers of audience engagement. Brands will focus on creating compelling video content to capture attention in an increasingly competitive digital landscape.

d) Voice Search Optimisation: As voice search continues to grow in popularity, optimising content for voice search will become essential. Marketers will need to adapt their content strategies to accommodate voice-based queries and ensure their content is discoverable through voice-enabled devices and platforms.

e) Sustainable and Purpose-Driven Content: Consumers are increasingly drawn to brands that align with their values and demonstrate a commitment to social and environmental causes. Content marketing will reflect this shift, with brands focusing on creating purpose-driven content that resonates with socially conscious audiences.

f) Immersive Technologies: Augmented reality (AR) and virtual reality (VR) will open up new possibilities for immersive content experiences. Brands will leverage these technologies to create interactive and engaging content that transports audiences to virtual environments, driving deeper engagement and emotional connections.

g) User-Generated Content (UGC) Amplification: UGC will continue to play a significant role in content marketing strategies. Brands will increasingly amplify UGC through social media channels, leveraging the authentic voices of their customers to build trust and credibility with their audience.

h) Data Privacy and Consent: With growing concerns around data privacy and regulation, marketers will need to prioritize transparency and consent in their content marketing practices. Building trust with consumers by respecting their privacy preferences will be crucial for maintaining positive brand relationships.

i) AI-Powered Content Creation: Artificial intelligence (AI) will streamline content creation processes, from content ideation and creation to distribution and optimization. AI-powered tools will enable marketers to analyse data, predict trends, and personalize content at scale, driving efficiency and effectiveness in content marketing campaigns.

j) Omnichannel Integration: As consumer touchpoints continue to expand across various channels and devices, brands will focus on creating seamless omnichannel experiences. Integrating content across multiple channels and platforms will be essential for delivering consistent messaging and engaging audiences wherever they are.

C. Reflection on the Dynamic Nature of the Digital Landscape

In today's rapidly evolving digital landscape, one cannot help but marvel at the dynamic nature of the space. From emerging technologies to shifting consumer behaviours, the digital realm is in a constant state of flux, presenting both opportunities and challenges for marketers.

One of the most striking aspects of the digital landscape is its relentless pace of change. What was considered innovative and cutting-edge yesterday may quickly become outdated tomorrow. This fast-paced environment demands agility and adaptability from marketers, requiring them to stay abreast of the latest trends and technologies to remain competitive.

Moreover, the digital landscape is characterised by its complexity and interconnectedness. The proliferation of channels, platforms, and devices has created a fragmented media landscape, making it increasingly challenging to reach and engage audiences effectively. Marketers must navigate this complexity by adopting an omnichannel approach, ensuring seamless integration across multiple touchpoints to deliver cohesive and personalised experiences to consumers.

At the heart of the digital landscape lies data – vast volumes of data generated by consumers' interactions and behaviours online. Data is the lifeblood of digital marketing, providing valuable insights into audience preferences, trends, and performance metrics. However, harnessing the power of data requires more than just collecting information – it requires a deep understanding of data analytics and the ability to derive actionable insights that drive informed decision-making.

Yet, amid the constant flux and complexity of the digital landscape, one thing remains constant: the importance of creativity and innovation. In an environment where attention spans are fleeting and competition is fierce, creativity is the key to standing out and capturing audience attention. Marketers must continually push the boundaries of creativity, experimenting with new formats, storytelling techniques, and interactive experiences to captivate audiences and drive engagement.

As we reflect on the dynamic nature of the digital landscape, we are reminded of the ever-present need for curiosity, adaptability, and a willingness to embrace change. By staying curious, keeping pace with technological advancements, and fostering a culture of innovation, marketers can navigate the complexities of the digital landscape and seize the opportunities that lie ahead.

## III. Encouragement for Continued Growth and Innovation

### A. Embracing a Culture of Continuous Learning and Adaptation

Embracing a culture of continuous learning and adaptation is imperative in navigating the dynamic digital landscape. As technologies evolve and consumer behaviours shift, marketers must remain agile and proactive in their approach. This involves fostering a mindset of curiosity and a willingness to explore new ideas and experiment with innovative strategies. By prioritising continuous learning, marketers can stay ahead of the curve, acquiring new skills and knowledge that enable them to adapt to emerging trends and technologies. Moreover, embracing adaptation means being open to change and flexible in responding to evolving market dynamics. This requires a willingness to reassess strategies, pivot when necessary, and embrace new opportunities as they arise. Ultimately, by cultivating a culture of continuous learning and adaptation, marketers can position themselves for long-term success in the ever-changing digital landscape.

B. Importance of Experimentation and Iterative Optimisation

A philosophy of iterative optimisation involves testing hypotheses, analysing results, and refining strategies based on data-driven insights. By embracing failure as a learning opportunity and iterating on successes, organisations can drive continuous improvement and innovation.

C. Motivation to Stay Ahead of the Curve and Embrace Change

The motivation to stay ahead of the curve and embrace change stems from a deep understanding of the dynamic nature of the digital landscape and its impact on marketing success. Recognising that stagnation is the enemy of progress, marketers are driven by a desire to remain relevant and competitive in an ever-evolving environment. By embracing change, marketers can position themselves as pioneers rather than followers, seizing opportunities for innovation and growth. Moreover, the thrill of navigating uncharted territories and pioneering new strategies fuels their motivation to push boundaries and challenge the status quo. Ultimately, the pursuit of staying ahead of the curve is not just about keeping up with the latest trends; it is about embracing a mindset of curiosity, adaptability, and resilience that empowers marketers to thrive in the face of uncertainty and change.

IV. Call to Action for Implementing Strategies

## A. Empowering Readers to Apply Strategies and Tactics Discussed in the Book

To translate theoretical knowledge into actionable strategies and tactics in content marketing, consider the following practical guidance, tips, and tools:

a) Content Calendar Template: Provide readers with a customisable content calendar template to plan and organise their content creation schedule effectively. This tool helps readers stay consistent with their publishing cadence and ensures alignment with overarching marketing objectives.

b) SEO Best Practices Guide: Offer practical tips and guidelines for optimising content for search engines. This includes keyword research techniques, on-page optimisation strategies, and advice on creating SEO-friendly content structures to improve visibility and organic traffic.

c) Social Media Management Tools: Introduce readers to social media management platforms such as Hootsuite or Buffer, which streamline the process of scheduling, publishing, and analysing social media content. These tools enable readers to maintain a consistent presence across various social channels and track engagement metrics efficiently.

d) Content Performance Analytics: Encourage readers to leverage analytics platforms like Google Analytics or HubSpot to monitor the performance of their content. Provide guidance on interpreting key metrics such as traffic sources, engagement rates, and conversion data to inform content optimization efforts.

e) Content Ideation Frameworks: Share frameworks and methodologies for generating content ideas that resonate with target audiences. This could include brainstorming exercises, audience persona mapping, or trend analysis techniques to uncover relevant topics and themes.

f) A/B Testing Toolkit: Educate readers on the importance of A/B testing and provide guidance on setting up experiments to optimize content performance. Offer recommendations for A/B testing tools and methodologies to refine content strategies based on empirical data and insights.

g) Email Marketing Automation Platforms: Introduce readers to email marketing automation platforms like Mailchimp or ConvertKit, which enable personalised email campaigns and automated workflows. Provide tips on segmentation, drip campaigns, and email optimisation to drive engagement and conversions.

h) Content Creation Resources: Curate a list of resources such as stock photo websites, design tools, and content creation guides to assist readers in producing high-quality visuals and multimedia content.

B. Encouragement for Taking Action and Implementing Content Marketing Initiatives

Now that you've gained valuable insights and equipped yourself with practical guidance, tips, and tools, it's time to take action and implement your content marketing initiatives. Remember, the true value of knowledge lies in its application. Don't be afraid to step out of your comfort zone and experiment with new strategies. Embrace the journey of learning and iteration, knowing that each step you take brings you closer to your goals.

Keep in mind that perfection is not the goal; progress is. Start small, test your ideas, and learn from both your successes and failures. Be adaptable and willing to pivot when necessary, but above all, be persistent. Rome wasn't built in a day, and neither is a successful content marketing strategy. Stay focused on your objectives, and don't lose sight of the bigger picture.

Moreover, remember that you're not alone on this journey. Reach out to your peers, mentors, and industry experts for support and guidance.

Collaboration and knowledge-sharing can often lead to innovative solutions and breakthroughs. And don't forget to celebrate your wins along the way, no matter how small they may seem. Each milestone achieved is a testament to your hard work and dedication.

So, take that first step, and let the journey begin. By implementing your content marketing initiatives with passion, perseverance, and a willingness to learn, you'll be well on your way to achieving your goals and making a meaningful impact in the digital landscape.

## C. Resources and Support for Your Content Marketing Journey

a) Online Communities and Forums: Join online communities and forums dedicated to content marketing where you can connect with fellow marketers, ask questions, and share experiences. Platforms like Reddit's r/content_marketing or LinkedIn groups provide valuable opportunities for networking and knowledge-sharing.

b) Industry Blogs and Publications: Follow industry-leading blogs and publications that offer insights, best practices, and case studies on content marketing. Websites like Content Marketing Institute, HubSpot Blog, and Moz provide a wealth of resources and educational content to support your learning journey.

c) Webinars and Workshops: Attend webinars, workshops, and virtual events hosted by industry experts and thought leaders. These interactive sessions offer opportunities to dive deeper into specific topics, ask questions, and gain practical skills through hands-on exercises and demonstrations.

d) Online Courses and Certifications: Enrol in online courses and certifications that cover various aspects of content marketing, from content strategy and creation to SEO and analytics. Platforms like Coursera, Udemy, and HubSpot Academy offer comprehensive courses taught by industry professionals.

e) Mentorship Programs: Seek mentorship from experienced professionals in the field who can provide personalised guidance, feedback, and support as you navigate your content marketing journey. Mentorship programs offered by professional organisations or networking groups can be invaluable resources for career development and growth.

f) Coaching and Consultation Services: Consider hiring a content marketing coach or consultant to provide tailored advice, strategies, and accountability in achieving your content marketing goals. These professionals offer personalized support and expertise to help you overcome challenges and achieve success.

g) Professional Associations and Networking Events: Join professional associations and attend networking events, conferences, and meetups related to content marketing. These platforms provide opportunities to learn from industry experts, build connections, and stay updated on the latest trends and developments in the field.

h) Online Tools and Software: Utilize online tools and software to streamline your content marketing efforts and enhance productivity. From content management systems (CMS) and analytics platforms to design tools and social media management software, leveraging the right tools can simplify tasks and improve efficiency in your workflow.

## V. Acknowledgment and Gratitude

### A. Thanking Contributors, Mentors, and Inspirations

I extend my heartfelt gratitude to the contributors, mentors, and inspirations who have played pivotal roles in shaping our content marketing journey. Special thanks to Sarah Garcia, whose insightful contributions and expertise have enriched my understanding of content strategy and audience engagement. I am immensely grateful to MRP for their unwavering support and guidance as mentors, offering valuable advice and encouragement every step of the way. Additionally, we are inspired by the innovative work of industry leaders such as Bob Proctor, whose groundbreaking campaigns and thought leadership continue to motivate me to push the boundaries of creativity and excellence in content marketing. To all those who have shared their knowledge, offered guidance, and served as beacons of inspiration, we express our deepest appreciation. Your contributions have been instrumental in shaping our journey and empowering us to achieve our goals in the ever-evolving digital landscape.

### B. Expressing Gratitude for the Opportunity to Share Knowledge and Insights

I am immensely grateful for the opportunity to share knowledge and insights in the dynamic realm of content marketing. It has been a privilege to contribute to the collective wisdom of the community and to inspire others on their own content marketing journey.

Special thanks to all the readers, learners, and collaborators who have engaged with our content, challenged our perspectives, and enriched the dialogue with their valuable contributions. We are grateful for the trust and support you have extended to us, allowing us to be part of your learning and growth. It is through this shared exchange of ideas and experiences that we continue to evolve and innovate in the ever-changing landscape of digital marketing.

In conclusion, reflecting on the evolution of content marketing, discussing emerging trends and future directions, encouraging continued growth and innovation, issuing a call to action for implementing strategies, expressing acknowledgment and gratitude, the author aims to inspire readers to embrace change, take action, and drive positive outcomes in their content marketing journey.

## VII. Conclusion: Empowering Readers to Make an Impact

## A. Final Thoughts and Words of Encouragement

As you continue your own content marketing journey, remember that every challenge is an opportunity for growth, every setback is a chance to learn, and every success is a testament to your dedication and resilience. Embrace change with open arms, stay curious, and never underestimate the power of your voice and ideas. You have the potential to make a lasting impact, to inspire others, and to shape the future of content marketing. So, forge ahead with confidence, passion, and purpose. The world awaits your brilliance, and we are excited to see where your journey takes you. Remember, the best is yet to come.

## B. In Summary

In summary, our journey through the dynamic landscape of content marketing has been marked by discovery, collaboration, and growth. From exploring emerging trends and future directions to providing practical guidance and tools, we've strived to empower our readers to navigate the complexities of the digital realm with confidence and purpose. As we close this chapter, we leave you with a message of encouragement: embrace change, stay curious, and never underestimate the power of your ideas. Your journey in content marketing is just beginning, and the opportunities for innovation and impact are boundless. Remember, the key to success lies not only in what you know but in how you apply that knowledge to create meaningful connections and drive results. With determination, resilience, and a commitment to continuous learning, you have the power to shape the future of content marketing and make a lasting difference in the digital landscape.

## Glossary

**A**

**Analytics:** The practice of analysing data to gain insights into audience behaviour, content performance, and marketing effectiveness, often using tools such as Google Analytics or social media analytics platforms.

**Audience Engagement:** The level of interaction, participation, and connection between a brand's content and its target audience.

**B**

**Call to Action (CTA):** A prompt or instruction that encourages users to take a specific action, such as clicking a button, filling out a form, or making a purchase.

**C**

**Content Calendar:** A schedule or plan that outlines the dates, topics, and formats for upcoming content releases, helping to maintain consistency and organisation in content marketing efforts.

**Content Marketing:** A strategic marketing approach focused on creating and distributing valuable, relevant, and consistent content to attract and engage a target audience.

**Conversion Rate:** The percentage of website visitors or content viewers who take a desired action, such as making a purchase, signing up for a newsletter, or completing a form.

**E**

**Engagement Metrics:** Key performance indicators (KPIs) used to measure the level of interaction and participation with content, including likes, shares, comments, clicks, and time spent on page.

**O**

**Omnichannel Marketing:** A marketing approach that ensures seamless integration and consistency across multiple channels and touchpoints, providing customers with a unified and cohesive experience.

## P

**Persona:** A fictional representation of a target audience segment, based on demographic, psychographic, and behavioural characteristics, used to tailor content and marketing strategies.

**Personalisation:** The practice of tailoring content, offers, and experiences to individual preferences, interests, and behaviours, enhancing relevance and engagement.

## S

**SEO (Search Engine Optimisation):** The process of optimising a website or content to improve its visibility and ranking in search engine results pages (SERPs), thereby increasing organic traffic.

**Social Media Management:** The process of planning, creating, scheduling, publishing, and analysing content across social media platforms to engage and interact with an audience.

## U

**User-Generated Content (UGC):** Content created and shared by users or customers, often in the form of reviews, testimonials, photos, or videos, which can be leveraged by brands to build trust and authenticity.

# Index

## A

A/B Testing · 39, 43, 50, 76, 86, 95, 110, 131, 145, 203
Audience Analysis · 88
Audience Behaviour · 45, 129, 132
Audience Engagement · 1, 3, 11, 20, 52, 53, 65, 70, 79, 119, 152, 174, 196, 208
Audience Personas · 32, 33, 139
Audience Understanding · 30, 47, 50, 117

## B

Behavioural Segmentation · 31, 68, 104, 129
Brand Voice Consistency · 41, 141

## C

Case Studies · 13, 24, 47, 48, 85, 113, 146, 167, 188
Content Creation · 25, 40, 56, 59, 65, 69, 77, 86, 123, 140, 178, 183, 199, 203
Content Formats · 7, 9, 60, 83, 174, 197
Content Management Systems (CMS) · 75, 123, 142, 144
Content Marketing · 1, 2, 5, 7, 11, 12, 13, 14, 17, 18, 20, 22, 23, 24, 25, 26, 27, 28, 29, 30, 48, 50, 51, 58, 137, 143, 152, 173, 181, 182, 184, 186, 193, 195, 196, 197, 203, 204, 208
Content Messaging · 40, 141
Content Optimisation · 52, 179
Content Performance Metrics · 44
Content Personalisation · 142
Content Strategies · 42, 45, 67, 72, 76, 77, 78
Conversion Metrics · 45, 75, 91
Customer Feedback · 35, 37, 103, 154, 161
Customer Surveys · 32

## D

Data Analysis · 42, 50, 76, 138, 145, 166
Delivery Channels · 60, 61
Demographic Analysis · 31
Demographic Segmentation · 68, 103
Distribution Channels · 15, 79, 83

## E

Email Marketing Platforms · 93, 124
Engagement Metrics · 45, 74, 90, 93, 118, 119, 120, 122, 133, 144, 208
Evaluating Content Performance · 74
Evolution of Content Marketing · 5, 197

## G

Google Analytics · 26, 35, 36, 75, 92, 94, 109, 121, 122, 127, 145, 166, 202, 208

## M

Measuring Engagement · 15, 117

## P

Personalised Content · 67, 77, 149, 197

Psychographic Profiling · 31

## R

Real-World Examples · 47, 113, 132, 167
Resources and Tools · 25

## S

Social Media Analytics · 35, 75, 93, 110, 122

## T

Tools and Resources · 36, 67
Trends and Challenges · 7

## U

User-Generated Content · 6, 7, 10, 72, 73, 77, 111, 115, 164, 198, 209

## V

Visual Content · 65, 67, 83, 177
Visualisation · 128, 179

www.ingramcontent.com/pod-product-compliance
Lightning Source LLC
Chambersburg PA
CBHW071206240526
45470CB00018B/1517